THE
CULTURE
QUESTION

THE
CULTURE
QUESTION

HOW TO CREATE A WORKPLACE
WHERE PEOPLE LIKE TO WORK

RANDY GRIESER, ERIC STUTZMAN
WENDY LOEWEN, MICHAEL LABUN

ACHIEVE
PUBLISHING

Published by ACHIEVE Publishing
120 Sherbrook Street, Winnipeg, Manitoba R3C 2B4
www.achievecentre.com

ACHIEVE
PUBLISHING

Bulk discounts available. For details contact:
ACHIEVE Publishing at 1-877-270-9776 or info@achievecentre.com

This book is typeset in Adobe Garamond Pro and Proxima Nova.
Printed with vegetable-based inks on 100% PCW paper.

ISBN: 978-1-988617-08-4
ISBN: 978-1-988617-09-1 (e-book)

Printed and bound in Canada
First edition, first printing

Book design by Ninth and May Design Co.

10 9 8 7 6 5 4 3 2 1

To our staff, colleagues, and clients,
who have taught us so much.
This book would not exist without you.

Contents

Introduction

LIKING WHERE WE WORK

We believe that people should be able to like where they work. When employees like the places they work, it's not only good for their mental health and well-being, it's also good for their organizations – both financially and otherwise. When a workplace culture is purposefully created to be respectful and inspiring, employees are happier, more productive, and more engaged.

Unfortunately, far too many people don't like where they work. Some organizations are unhealthy and full of disrespectful behavior. Other workplaces are simply uninspiring. For various reasons, countless people feel trapped, indifferent, or bored at work.

Our organization, ACHIEVE, provides training and resources that give people insights and tools for creating, cultivating, and sustaining workplaces that are respectful, engaging, and meaningful. To teach others effectively, we have needed to consistently nurture an environment in our workplace that reflects the principles we speak about. When clients walk into our office, we want them to see that we actually "walk the talk" and our belief in the value of a healthy and likable workplace culture is authentic.

We have worked hard to create a healthy culture, choosing to learn from our mistakes and from the wisdom of others. We are now passionate about helping people create great workplaces, and that is why we've written this book – to help create workplaces where people like to work.

The title of this book, *The Culture Question*, may have led you to ask, "What's the question?" In short, the fundamental question has two parts: "How does your organization's culture impact how much people like where they work?" and "What can you do to make it better?" In this book, we help you answer these questions by focusing on the elements that make up a healthy workplace culture.

WHO THIS BOOK IS FOR

If you've picked up *The Culture Question*, there's a good chance that you are not happy with your organization's culture, or perhaps you think it could at least be better than it is now.

If you know deep down that there is a better way, that things don't have to stay the same, this book is for you.

If you see glimpses of what might be, but you're not sure how to influence culture change in your workplace, this book is for you.

If you are one of those fortunate individuals who works in an organization that has a strong culture, but you are unsure how to maintain that strength as you grow, change, and face the future, this book is for you.

If you are a leader who wants to consciously cultivate a healthy organizational culture, this book is for you.

Leadership bears much responsibility for the health of an organization's culture, but everyone in the organization has a role in impacting and sustaining that culture. Throughout this book, we use "leaders" in an inclusive sense to refer to all of those who influence others in the workplace. This book will be applicable for supervisors, managers, human resources personnel, union representatives, executives, and others who provide leadership in an organization.

WHAT LIES AHEAD

The insights found in this book have emerged out of the learning opportunities we have had within our own workplace and alongside the countless other organizations we have supported and worked with.

As well as drawing on these experiences and other research, we have also conducted "The Culture Question Survey," which includes perspectives from over 2,400 participants about what does and does not make a great place to work.[1] We asked both employees and leaders to identify whether they like where they work, and then correlated their responses to a series of statements about workplace culture. We were amazed by the survey results and are thankful for the number of people who took the time to thoughtfully provide their opinions and perspectives. Results, insights, and quotes from the survey are woven into the following chapters and provide additional depth to the book. A more detailed analysis can be found in the Survey Analysis section on page 182.

The first chapter of this book makes the case that organizational culture should be a priority for every workplace. The remaining chapters are each about a particular aspect of creating, transforming, and sustaining a healthy workplace culture. At the end of each chapter, we've included questions you can use either for personal reflection or for larger group discussions. The Resources section at the end of the book provides additional examples and actionable tools you can use within your own organization.

We are aware that not every aspect of this book will apply directly to every reader. Our goal is not so much to provide a "cookie cutter" blueprint, but rather to give you guidelines and inspiration as you work toward creating and sustaining a culture where people like to work.

Ultimately, our goal in writing this book is to reduce the suffering that so many people experience at work and thus increase our collective well-being. We want to do our part to create a world in which everyone has the opportunity to experience the joy of liking where they work.

The Case for Caring About Culture

FOCUS ON CULTURE, NOT FOOSBALL

Most of us are familiar with stories from some of the "best" places to work – the Googles of the world, with their complimentary food courts, fancy buildings, free massages, and foosball tables. Decision makers at many of these companies likely feel that these extra perks help make their organizations great places to work and that they will attract and retain talented, motivated, and productive employees as a result.

These initiatives sound great, and they may indeed help create more fun and productive organizations. However, the reality is that most of our workplaces do not have the resources to implement these sorts of programs. The good news is that, while these types of perks may be nice, they aren't actually necessary for attracting productive and committed employees who enjoy their work and are loyal to their organizations. Instead, the key is building a healthy workplace culture.

Culture must be your highest priority if you want to make your organization a great place to work. Even if game rooms and free gourmet food are options for your organization, perks alone will not create a healthy culture if you do not also consider the priorities we outline in the next six chapters:

- **Communicating your purpose and values.** Employees are inspired when they work in organizations whose purpose and values resonate with them.
- **Providing meaningful work.** Most employees want to work on projects that inspire them, align with what they are good at, and allow them to grow.
- **Focusing your leadership team on people.** How leaders relate to their employees plays a major role in how everyone feels about their workplace.
- **Building meaningful relationships.** When employees like the people they work with and for, they are more satisfied and more engaged in their work.
- **Creating peak performing teams.** People are energized when they work together effectively because teams achieve things that no one person could do on their own.
- **Practicing constructive conflict management.** When leaders don't handle conflict promptly and well, it quickly sours the workplace.

The chapters that follow will explore each of these areas in more depth. We will demonstrate the importance of directing your energy toward each key area, and we will offer some practical ways for your organization to build these six priorities into your workplace culture.

WHAT IS CULTURE?

Workplace culture is the most significant factor that influences happiness, work relationships, and job satisfaction. Having a clear understanding of what workplace culture is, and what your own organization's culture is, will help you more easily identify problems and develop strategies to create a better culture and capitalize on its positive energy.

In their *Harvard Business Review* (*HBR*) article "The Leader's Guide to Corporate Culture," Boris Groysberg and others write:

Culture is the tacit social order of an organization: It shapes attitudes and behaviors in wide-ranging and durable ways. Cultural norms define what is encouraged, discouraged, accepted, or rejected within a group. When properly aligned with personal values, drives, and needs, culture can unleash tremendous amounts of energy toward a shared purpose and foster an organization's capacity to thrive.[1]

Though organizational culture isn't a physical thing, you feel it every day in the ways you work and engage with others. Culture is represented in the language you use, the stories you tell, and your daily work practices. Simple things, like the objects hanging on an office wall, can tell you a lot about an organization's culture. Whether you are walking to get a coffee, attending a meeting, or eating lunch, culture is present.

Workplace cultures include elements such as values, mission statements, leadership styles, and expectations for how employees treat customers, clients, and each other. Culture is visible through the ways in which people interact with each other – *their behaviors*. It is reflected in how things get done. It is made up of the principles and rituals that hold an organization together.

Each organization has its own distinct "personality." Much like an individual's personality, it is related to the collective values, beliefs, and attitudes of its members. No two workplace cultures are the same. In fact, culture is the one thing that makes each organization unique. Products and strategies can be replicated, but a culture is as distinct as a fingerprint.

For simplicity, we often refer to organizational culture as "unhealthy" or "healthy." However, workplaces are almost never all good or all bad. Instead, they exist on a spectrum of *less* healthy to *more* healthy.

In organizations on the unhealthy end of the spectrum, people are usually less motivated and may be influenced by an element of fear that can drag down their productivity. In healthier cultures, people have a sense of empowerment that energizes and inspires them to perform at a higher level. Healthy cultures create a sense of belonging, purpose, and engagement, which ultimately drives desired behaviors and results.

Two of our survey participants summarized their workplace cultures in the following ways:

- "We have a great team and a strong vision. Our manager is amazing and gives us freedom to try new things. I feel like I am making a difference in the lives of the people I work with. I am able to use my gifts and talents in ways that make me feel valuable and useful. I love my job, my boss, and my coworkers!"
- "My coworkers are kind and caring people. I have autonomy in what I do but receive enough direction that it's not overwhelming. There is clear purpose to the mundane tasks and enough exciting tasks to keep me engaged. Overall, it's the best work environment I've had the chance to be in."

These two statements highlight key elements found in many healthy workplaces. Although these survey participants may wish to improve some aspects of their workplaces, they clearly work in organizations on the healthier end of the culture spectrum.

WHY CULTURE MATTERS

Focusing on creating a workplace culture where people *want* to work is simply the right thing to do. But there are also practical and financial reasons for investing energy into organizational culture. In a survey conducted by Duke's Fuqua School of Business, and completed by 1,400 North American CEOs, executives overwhelmingly indicated that a healthy corporate culture is essential if an organization is to thrive.[2]

During the Industrial Revolution, it was likely more feasible to build a profitable business without taking culture into account. Standardizing tasks and eliminating errors were usually enough to make a company profitable. How employees felt about their workplace was less important to an organization's sustainability than the ability to get work done in a timely and efficient manner. However, when we consider the social unrest of the industrial societies of the past, it is clear that many people were profoundly unhappy.

The type of work that many people do today is very different from work that was done in the past. Fewer people produce goods, which can easily be measured in terms of productivity, while more people provide services, which are difficult to quantify. To maintain productivity in most of today's work environments, which require innovation and collaboration, we need healthy work cultures.

In our consulting work, we have seen the very real financial *and* human costs associated with unhealthy workplace cultures. Financially, the costs of an unhealthy organizational culture include high turnover and an unproductive, unengaged work force. When it comes to the human costs, people's mental health and overall well-being suffer. We believe that organizations that don't focus on creating healthy workplace cultures will eventually be replaced by those that do.

OUR WORKPLACE CULTURE

Our organization has two primary divisions: ACHIEVE Centre for Leadership & Workplace Performance (ACHIEVE), and the Crisis & Trauma Resource Institute (CTRI), which provides training and resources in the areas of mental health, counseling skills, and violence prevention. For simplicity, we refer to our organization as ACHIEVE in this book. Though it took us some time to develop a healthy culture, we're proud that our own organization is a place where people like to work. We do great work, we are energized by what we do, and we also laugh and have a lot of fun. Most of the time, invigorating energy permeates our workplace. People are excited about being innovative and productive while doing meaningful work.

If you visit our office, you will find our culture at work. You will see inspirational quotes and pictures on the wall, you will hear energetic bursts of chatter about ideas, and you will smell good coffee – because good coffee makes having a great culture easier, right? If you attend our meetings, you will see employees who are not afraid to speak up or disagree with leaders. You might even notice some frustration from time to time, often caused because we care when things don't go right.

For this portion of the book, we asked some of the staff at ACHIEVE to identify the things they like about our workplace. These are some of their responses:

- "Mostly the people – I love my coworkers. They make it easy to come to work."
- "I have freedom and autonomy in how I do my work."
- "Leadership values my abilities and the work I do."
- "I find my work meaningful. I love that I get to help people."
- "I get to do new things, and I am challenged by my work."
- "Leadership includes me in decisions that impact the organization."

These responses provide insight into what's important for creating a healthy and vibrant workplace culture. Our staff like the people they work with and the environment they work in. They value communication and teamwork. They appreciate that we, as leaders, value their work and communicate effectively. Our team members find their work challenging and meaningful and, most importantly, they connect with the purpose of our organization.

Our culture has not always been healthy, and we have had to learn some important lessons along the way. There was a time when we didn't communicate our purpose to our staff as clearly as we should have. We hired people who negatively impacted our culture, and we allowed conflict to escalate to the point that it became unhealthy.

Early on in our organization's history, in one of our unhealthier periods, things were bad enough that we needed to make major changes. We were a much smaller organization then, and leadership was focused on the many pressing *operational matters* rather than the health of relationships and the organization's culture. As a result, what started as differences of opinion and conflicting work styles escalated into high levels of distrust and disrespect among staff. Productivity and communication plummeted, and it soon became clear that *organizational health* was now the pressing matter that demanded our attention.

Over a period of several months, we used many of the approaches we describe in this book. We gathered information using an assessment tool, we met with and listened to staff individually and in focus groups, and provided coaching and mediation. Unfortunately, we had to terminate one employee who wasn't willing to participate in the process, but it was a necessary step as we began building a healthier culture.

These past experiences have taught us to place a high value on our workplace's culture. Because it is so important to us, we ask each employee and manager, during their yearly goal-setting meetings, to comment on how they contribute to a positive workplace culture. We ask potential new hires what they will do to foster a healthy work environment. We see every person as a contributor to our culture, and we see our leaders as curators of our culture who intentionally think about how to keep it healthy.

YOUR WORKPLACE CULTURE

Because of the type of work we do at ACHIEVE, we regularly have the opportunity to walk through a variety of organizations. We've learned how to quickly assess workplace cultures based on the greetings we receive, the stories people tell, and the conversations we hear – or more importantly, don't hear.

Through our experiences, we have observed that most organizations are actually *okay* places to work. Yes, some workplaces are on the extreme ends of the spectrum – some are exceptional organizations that people love to be part of, and others are entirely toxic and dysfunctional. But most workplaces fall somewhere between these two extremes. They are *okay, but not great*. Most workplace cultures have some parts that are healthy and others that aren't as healthy.

When you tell others about your organization, what descriptors come to mind? To what extent is your workplace healthy or unhealthy? What parts of it are engaging and likable, and what parts are not? When other people walk into your workspace, what do you think they sense about your culture?

'How Do Things Really Work Around Here?'

While working in another organization early in my career, I, Randy, was approached by a new employee a week into his job. He came to me in a private manner, leaned in, and whispered, "So how do things really work around here?" What he was really asking was, "What's the culture of this place?" He wanted to know what the dos and don'ts were, whether leaders were authentic and what was important to them, whether people were really as nice as they seemed, and what it was he needed to watch out for.

We should really *all* be asking that question, not just new hires. *How do things really work around here?*

PRIORITIZING CULTURE

Although some organizations continuously prioritize workplace culture, many only give it occasional attention, if any at all. In our view, building and sustaining a great workplace culture requires intention, time, and effort.

The challenge is that most of us are already working at full capacity in our other areas of responsibility. Working on culture often takes a back seat to things like strategic planning or marketing. It is something we think we will get to when these other tasks are taken care of. Ironically, when organizations put too much energy into products and profit at the expense of culture, their bottom line usually suffers. But if we take time to develop a healthy workplace culture *first*, we can capitalize on the energy it creates, and our other tasks become easier as a result.

The good news is that culture is something we can influence. We have little control over factors like government policy, demographics, or the economy, but we can influence our own workplaces in significant ways.

It is paramount that you recognize that culture is the essential ingredient in the glue holding your organization together. Culture is what determines whether your organization will succeed – or even survive. It has profound effects both on the quality of the products or services you provide and on the lives of those who work in your organization.

QUESTIONS FOR REFLECTION

1. Does your organization have a culture where people like to work? How do you know?
2. What would someone think about your culture if they could observe it unnoticed? What would a visitor walking through your workspace see and hear? What would this tell them about your culture?
3. When you and your colleagues describe your organization, what words and stories do you use? What does this tell you about your culture?

Communicate Your Purpose & Values

DOING WORK THAT MATTERS

One morning as I, Eric, left the house, I said to my preschool-aged daughter, "Have a fun day on your field trip!" She replied, "Have a fun day at work!" Her reply made me smile. It was such a natural response coming from a child. Who doesn't like to have fun? Yet I couldn't help thinking that, while I like to have fun at work, I don't go there specifically to have fun. Instead, I go because there is purpose in my work.

My work matters because it meets the needs of our clients and helps achieve our organizational purpose. In moment-to-moment ways, my work also makes a positive difference for my colleagues. This sense of purpose motivates me to come to the office each day and do good work.

At a fundamental level, one reason we all work is to earn a living so that we can meet our basic needs, such as food and shelter. However, once our physical needs are met, most of us desire something deeper from our work, like *meaning*. We want to matter and to see that our efforts make a positive difference.

Imagine if your work life consisted of a series of unending tasks with no connection to any purpose, like Sisyphus, from Greek mythology, who pushed a rock up a hill every day only to have it roll back down. What if your work didn't matter to anyone? Consider how this would affect your motivation to be at work. For most of us, it would be devastating.

The sense of doing work that matters often gets overlooked as a key factor for organizations in creating places where people like to work. Rather than intentionally defining and communicating their purpose, too many organizations emphasize completing tasks, accomplishing short-term goals, and even having fun, with the hope that these priorities will motivate people. While tasks, goals, and fun are significant, they need to be put in their proper place – in support of purpose.

Although we have long known that purpose matters for creating a healthy organizational culture, we were surprised by just how significant it was shown to be in our survey. Ninety-eight percent of survey participants who said they have a great workplace also agreed that their organization has a meaningful purpose! This is a huge indicator that healthy organizational cultures must be anchored to meaningful purpose.

In this chapter, we'll explore organizational purpose, team purpose, and individual purpose. We will also take a look at what it means to articulate authentic values. Purpose and values, whether we name them or not, significantly shape our workplace cultures. Organizations that don't spend time thinking about these things will be guided by unclear priorities. On the other hand, an organization that proactively names its purpose and values can shape and guide its culture to create the kind of workplace where people like to work.

SURVEY STATISTICS

My organization has a meaningful purpose.

According to our survey, 98 percent of people who like their workplace also believe their organization has a meaningful purpose.

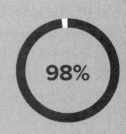

98%

PURPOSE: WHERE TO START

Organizations can articulate purpose on many levels, from the value of individual tasks and roles, to the significance of entire departments, to the overarching purpose of the organization as a whole. When we understand the purpose of something, we can choose to engage with it more deeply and freely or disengage with clarity about why we don't want to participate.

One way to understand purpose is to think about it as the *why* behind our actions. Many of us who have had young children in our lives know that, at about three years old, they start to ask "why?" *incessantly*. They want to know why we need to eat at particular times, why they have to wear pants outside the house, and why dogs and cats can be pets inside our homes, but not pigs or cows. Although we may not do it as incessantly as children (at least not out loud), we often still ask "why?" We are propelled to understand why we need to do things, why we should engage with them, and why they matter.

Before considering its divisions, departments, or individual job descriptions, every organization must first define its overarching purpose and articulate it as a clear and succinct mission statement. This mission statement will drive the work of the organization, and the purpose of every individual and team action must relate to it in some way. The key to naming purpose is to do it in a meaningful way.

Unfortunately, despite hours of hard work, some mission statements end up being uninspiring or failing to clearly describe purpose. We've seen many mission statements that read something like this: "As a partner to our clients, we aim to be number one in their minds when they think of our services." Or, "We aspire to maximize sales through innovative and quality products." The problem with these statements, of course, is that they are generic, lack meaning to the reader, and fail to inspire the day-to-day work of their organizations.

Other mission statements we've come across describe an organization's products, services, or goals, but say nothing about its purpose. For example, "Our mission is to be the number one auto-parts dealer in our region." This type of statement may be helpful for potential clients who want to understand what the company does, but it will not set that company apart from its competitors, and it is not likely to inspire staff or customers.

An effective mission statement will both explain why your organization exists and inspire and energize your leaders, employees, and clients. As Simon Sinek aptly states in his TED talk, "People don't buy *what* you do; they buy *why* you do it."[1] As you articulate purpose within your organization, remember that your audience, whether it's your employees, clients, or customers, should be able to understand the *why* behind your organization's actions.

HOW TO ARTICULATE ORGANIZATIONAL PURPOSE

Although culture change will happen most readily once everyone within an organization identifies with its purpose, articulating that purpose begins with leadership. If you're in a leadership role, it's your responsibility to get everyone else talking about purpose. You can use the following questions to start the conversation:

- **How is your organization making the world a better place?** Without a fundamental commitment to making the world a better place, organizations may develop substandard products and services or adopt unethical and predatory practices. If an organization's sole purpose is to enrich its owners or staff, it is far more likely that its ethics will drift toward self-interest to the detriment of the wider community.
- **Why does your particular organization exist?** The key to this question is to consider what makes your organization unique. Your answer should give people a reason to connect with your organization rather than another organization that provides similar products or services.
- **What are you trying to achieve in the big picture?** This question connects to your *why* by helping you focus on goals. Look beyond profit or service delivery metrics because these measurements are simply related to what you do, not why you do it.

The questions we've provided here are challenging but important. To give you some ideas of how an effective mission statement can define an organization's purpose, here are some examples:

- A hospital: "To provide a trusted place for community residents to seek healing."
- A car dealership: "To make it simple and stress-free to buy or sell a vehicle."
- A school: "To open the minds and hearts of children to a life of learning and growth."
- An insurance company: "To help people recover from life's hardships."

Our Mission

ACHIEVE's mission (our *why*) is to *inspire learning and improve lives*. At the heart of our workshop materials and resources lies a belief that people should be able to like where they work.

We are a provider of professional development training and workplace consulting services – that's *what* we do. We provide high-quality and accessible training and resources by hiring exceptional facilitators and carefully developing and testing our materials – that's *how* we do it. But *why* we do what we do is far more important and inspiring than the *what* and the *how*.

Our mission and belief drive everything we do. There are many other professional development training organizations, but what makes us unique is not simply the topics we teach or the ways in which we deliver our material. Rather, we are unique in how our particular belief informs how and why we do what we do.

We've learned the following key things by participating in and leading other organizations through conversations about purpose:

- **Conversations about purpose need time and space.** We encourage people to go somewhere that is free from day-to-day distractions to think about purpose. Discussing purpose requires dedicated time and intentional focus on what really matters to your organization and the people who work there.
- **Mission statements should be tested.** A true mission statement will resonate deeply not only with those who have articulated it but also with others throughout the organization, as well as external stakeholders and clients. Share your prospective mission statement with others and take note of their reactions. You'll know you have hit the mark when your statement provokes interest and excitement in others.
- **Mission statements rarely change.** Organizational vision may shift from time to time. Goals might be adjusted relative to the current environment, and methods need to change as society evolves. But while the language of a mission statement may change, its meaning rarely does – through it all, your organization's purpose acts as its foundation.
- **Mission statements are richer when tied to statements of belief.** Beliefs are convictions about the way things are or should be. Your beliefs make up a large part of what motivates your organization, and naming them can help others better understand your purpose. When discussing purpose, ask, "What do we believe to be true about the world, and how does that inform why we do what we do?"
- **Mission statements need connection to values.** As leaders articulate purpose, they also need to ask which values shape how they and others in their organization act. Core values, or DNA values (as we define them on page 28), outline where your organization will take a stand in terms of the ways it behaves or

won't behave. Values anchor action, and they offer another point of connection to your organization.

THE TEAM PURPOSE CONNECTION

Just as organizations get bad results when they are disconnected from a greater purpose, so do teams. In our consulting work, we have often observed that when teams don't connect with their organization's greater purpose, motivation and productivity suffer.

Team disconnection from organizational purpose often contributes to one of the greatest internal dangers an organization can face: the creation of "silos." Silos are isolated groups of workers that end up competing for resources rather than collaborating for the greater good. As teams build the walls of their silos, communication between them diminishes or gets funneled through leadership, sometimes erupting into unhealthy conflict.

For example, we've seen Information Technology departments that are so focused on keeping their organization's technology secure that they neglect to think creatively about providing tools to ensure the organization can efficiently achieve its greater mission. Instead of working together with those who are trying to innovate, they may constantly shut others down with worries about security. At the same time, other departments operating in their silos may resent the Information Technology department because they don't fully understand how tech security functions and see them as a barrier to innovation.

A team's purpose will never be identical to its organization's purpose because it will inevitably have a unique function within the organization. Given the specific priorities and responsibilities of each team, one of the most effective ways to prevent silos from forming is to ground each team's purpose in its relationship to the overarching purpose of the organization. If you are a team leader, you can use the following three questions to begin these conversations:

- **What is the work of your team, and why does it matter?** In the same way that organizations need to move beyond discussions about *what* they do, teams should also have a clear sense of the *relevance* of their work.
- **What would be lost if you didn't exist as a team?** This question is essentially the flip side of the first. We have found it useful because some people find it easier to understand purpose in this way.
- **How are you contributing to the work of other teams and the organization's purpose as a whole?** This question emphasizes what your team can provide to the organization rather than focusing on how it can get its own needs met. When each team focuses on contributing to the whole rather than competing for resources, the result is increased energy and synergy.

These questions provide clarity and meaning for teams while aligning them with the overall purpose of the organization. When teams identify with organizational purpose, they commit to the welfare of other teams and the organization as a whole.

THE INDIVIDUAL PURPOSE CONNECTION

In the same way that a pure profit motive divorced from a greater purpose leads to unhealthy organizational practices, so does working solely for a paycheck at an individual level. We have seen time and again how poorly people perform when all they care about – or all they have left to care about – is the paycheck at the end of the week.

When people have nothing deeper than a financial reward to engage them in their work, they are usually uninspired to contribute more than the minimal amount required to get paid or keep their job. Instead of focusing on how to make the world a better place through their work, they begin to focus on how to avoid unpleasant tasks, how many months they have left until retirement, or how to make their résumé look better to get a higher paying job.

One of the most significant reasons for articulating organizational purpose is that it allows individuals to connect their personal purpose to the organization's purpose. Organizational purpose should motivate staff and inspire individual action. Ultimately, we want people to engage with their work because their own *why* connects with the organization's *why*.

Individual engagement with the *why* of an organization provides meaning to people's work and brings a sense of connection and happiness. As Tony Hsieh writes in his book *Delivering Happiness*, "The combination of physical synchrony with other humans and being part of something bigger than oneself (and thus losing momentarily a sense of self) leads to a greater sense of happiness."[2] One of our survey participants wrote about their connection to their organization's purpose in this way: "My organization has a positive purpose. That counts for an awful lot. This is the only place I have ever worked where I feel no qualms about supporting the aims of this organization through my efforts."

Several years ago, when I, Wendy, was on maternity leave, I was approached about applying for a position with a social services agency. The role was to oversee a program called Healthy Moms and Babies. Initially, I was not interested, but when the board told me the details of the role, I couldn't help but get excited.

The job entailed providing weekly programming for mothers. I was free to structure the program however I liked as long as it covered the key areas of nutrition and development. Best of all, I could take my eight-month-old son along – he was the demonstration baby! It was too good to pass up. I was able to connect my excitement about being a mother to an organizational purpose of educating other young mothers. It was an immensely rewarding job!

When people are considering whether or not to work for an organization, they are frequently drawn to the mission of the organization because they want to be a part of something that aligns with their own sense of purpose. At ACHIEVE, we didn't specifically set out to attract great employees by articulating our organizational purpose, but we soon learned we were doing just that.

Over the past few years, we have noticed that when we conduct job interviews, many candidates mention that they were drawn to our organization by the way we describe our purpose and beliefs. When people connect with our purpose from the outset, they are more likely to be a natural fit within our workplace and reinforce the culture we want.

We don't want employees to have to guess about why their work matters or what the aim of their work is on a day-to-day basis. When a new employee starts, we intentionally discuss the purpose of their work as it relates to their team and the organization as a whole. In their first week on the job, we have new employees sit with someone from every department to learn how their colleagues' roles connect with their own work and the organization's mission. Then, at our three-month review and every annual goal-setting meeting thereafter, we discuss this reflection question as it relates to their role: "How are you contributing to our organization's purpose?"

As leaders, we should lead by example and know how our individual purpose connects to our organization's purpose. In their *HBR* article "From Purpose to Impact," Nick Craig and Scott A. Snook state that "fewer than 20 percent of leaders have a strong sense of their own individual purpose. Even fewer can distill their purpose into a concrete statement."[3] Although some leaders may know their organization's purpose, it is crucial that they are able to connect it to their own personal purpose as well. It is only after we make this connection for ourselves that we are able to help our employees do the same.

As a leader, you can use the following questions for your own personal reflection and to assist your staff:

- **What is important to you about the work you do?** This question helps individuals reflect on how they personally value their own work. Invariably, it also leads people to consider their impact on the world around them.
- **What would be lost for your clients and/or colleagues if you weren't here to do your work?** This question elicits reflection

about the value and relevance of an individual's work, particularly as it relates to the people they work with or serve.

- **How are you positively contributing to the work of your team or the organization as a whole?** Just as we want teams to consider how they contribute to the organization, we also want individuals to think about what they have to offer. This moves their attention away from personal benefits and self-interest toward the ways in which they make a positive difference.

When having these conversations with staff, leaders should also offer their own perspectives, as they may see additional ways in which an individual's work matters. In our discussions about individual purpose, we should seek to create alignment with organizational purpose. As we align individual purpose with the purpose of both the team and the organization, we prepare our organization to perform at a level where people are inspired. This propels our organization toward reaching our goals and fulfilling our mission.

COMMUNICATE YOUR ORGANIZATION'S PURPOSE

Developing an organizational mission statement will only help so much. Organizations must also *communicate* that purpose in meaningful ways to the people they wish to engage with, both internally and externally.

In the last few years at ACHIEVE, we have become much more intentional about regularly communicating our purpose. When we're having individual conversations at the start of meetings and when we're giving reports about our plans and visions, we frequently refer back to our organizational purpose. It can be as simple as saying, "Although this database project is tedious, sorting our contacts into categories will help us connect in more relevant ways with those who want to access our resources."

We believe that when we intentionally communicate *why* we do what we do, our staff more clearly see how their daily work fits into the bigger picture. They are also reminded that leadership values the tasks at hand – even the mundane ones.

One of the ways we build excitement around our purpose is by sharing stories of how our work has impacted others. For example, when we receive a thank-you call or email from a client, we often share it with everyone and emphasize how their appreciation affirms our purpose. These are powerful reminders of why we do the work we do. It is through these stories that we see the positive impact our work has on others.

It is also important to create intentional times and spaces to discuss how work being done aligns with organizational purpose. For instance, at the beginning of a new project, teams should discuss how it will contribute to the organizational purpose. At key points along the way, they should then review how their work is, or is not, continuing to be relevant. Likewise, policies and procedures should always be measured against their impact on the organization's mission.

It's not enough to have a mission statement describing your purpose. It's not enough to post the statement on your walls, and it's not even enough to periodically read it aloud. Your purpose, your reason for being, your *why*, must be something that everyone thinks about daily. Organizations that thrive do so largely because they have employees *and* leaders who believe in and align with their purpose. The purpose becomes ingrained in "how things really work around here."

Ironically, we have seen senior leaders in closed-door sessions become passionate about their organization's purpose only to leave the room and never discuss it with their staff. When organizational leaders keep purpose to themselves, they are missing an opportunity. They are failing to recognize that the best way to see their organization's purpose manifested is to ensure that everyone within the organization embraces and is proud of its purpose.

Staff are rarely inspired by their organization's purpose when their leader isn't passionate about it. Leaders must inspire people to rally around purpose. We need to be passionate about our purpose and share our excitement everywhere we can – particularly when we have opportunities to do so in person. We must express our pride in the ways we impact, and could impact, the world. When we do this effectively, we energize those around us to work toward a common goal.

Aligning Purpose

In the written responses to our survey, participants wrote in a multitude of ways about the importance of purpose for creating a healthy organizational culture.

Some survey participants wrote in broad terms, suggesting that purpose is simply intrinsic. When asked what makes their workplace great, many used phrases like these:

"The work contributes to a better society."
"What we do has purpose and gives deeper meaning to our lives."
"What we do really matters. That motivates me and gives me a sense of purpose in my work."

As the above quote suggests, it can be energizing when an individual's purpose aligns with that of their organization. Here are more examples:

"We do great work that aligns with my own personal values."
"The mission of the organization encompasses core values that resonate very closely with my own."
"It's not a job, it's a personal calling."

Other survey participants wrote more specifically about the role leadership plays in creating purpose. They told us they appreciated their leaders' efforts to communicate purpose through both word and deed:

"The leaders walk the talk."
"Leaders share a clear vision about the purpose of our shared work together."

While the quotes above suggest that leaders have an important impact on employees' sense of purpose, those participants who had negative things to say about their sense of purpose usually directed their frustrations toward their leaders:

> "There is a distinct lack of communication about what our purpose is."
> "The senior leadership contributes little to the sense of purpose."

Our survey participants were clear that alignment with a greater purpose contributes to their satisfaction and motivation at work. This shows us that it's very important for leaders to clearly understand and communicate organizational purpose.

WHAT IF YOUR ORGANIZATION DIDN'T EXIST?

Purpose should matter not only to employees. It should matter to our customers, clients, and the broader community as well. Every organization needs external people to be invested in its purpose in order to survive in the long run.

Throughout history, businesses, not-for-profits, and government agencies have come and gone. Some have been missed for a moment, but most have been quickly forgotten, soon to be replaced by a different organization offering a similar or better experience. In order to remain intact and relevant to others, we need to ask ourselves questions like these:

- Would anyone care – would anyone be upset or saddened – if our organization didn't exist?
- Is what we do important and valuable enough to clients that they would have an emotional reaction upon hearing that we were no longer here?

- Is there anything about what we do that is so special that it would be missed dearly? Would someone else be able to offer a similar product or service to easily fill the void we've left?

During the process of writing this book, we read the opening paragraphs of this section at one of our staff meetings. In the conversation that followed, we asked our employees to share from their perspectives why we matter and how others might feel if we didn't exist. To our delight, there was no shortage of answers. Our staff recalled important events and heartfelt conversations with clients that served as proof in their minds that we would be missed if we ceased to exist.

This was a simple but powerful exercise, and we encourage you to try it with your own organization. If those in your organization struggle to come up with significant answers, use it as an opportunity to consider what you might do to increase your positive impact. If significant responses easily come to mind, listen for ways in which your organization makes an impact that you may not have considered before.

CONNECT AT AN EMOTIONAL LEVEL

One of the secrets to creating and sustaining an organization that will stand the test of time is to matter in the *minds*, and more importantly, the *emotions*, of the people who access your products or services. We say *emotions* because most people make decisions about which products to buy and services to use based on feelings, not rational thought.

Although we may consider information about organizations and their products rationally, our decisions also get processed through the emotional centers of our brains. It is the "feel good" connection to a brand or organization that keeps customers coming back for more.

Consider how your favorite brands or services make you feel. In all likelihood, the brands you like most are the ones that make you feel something – you may enjoy their products, they may inspire you, or maybe they make you feel "cool." Think about how often people say things like, "I considered the options, but this one just *felt* right." It's not enough to rationally convince customers that your product or service is the best. You must also make them feel that it is the right product or service for them.

Unfortunately, most organizations value logic over emotions. They don't often consider how people *feel* about their mission, products, or services on an emotional level. And yet it is only when we access and assess the emotions of our clients that we can truly answer the questions: "Do we really matter? Would anyone care if we didn't exist?"

If you are struggling to answer these questions affirmatively, spend time considering what you can do to matter in people's minds *and* hearts. Consider what can set you apart. Think about what can make your services or products valuable enough that they can't easily be replaced. Your answers will relate to your purpose. They will also lead you to your strategy for sustainability and success.

Find ways to listen to your clients and customers directly as well. Ask for their feedback regarding your mission and products or services. Listen to what people say on social media and websites where your products or services are reviewed. Thank people for their feedback and take action when you need to make something right.

Organizations that last, and even grow, do so because their customers and clients care deeply about them on an emotional level. They have clients who resonate with their services or products and, more importantly, connect emotionally with their purpose.

ORGANIZATIONAL VALUES

For a vehicle to do its job, it needs both an engine for power and a steering system so it can be guided. An organization is no different: its purpose is the engine that propels it forward, and its values are the steering system by which it is guided.

Purpose defines *why* you do what you do, and values define *how* you act in service of that purpose. Values are a key component of a healthy workplace culture because they clarify how your organization and its staff should behave. They provide the framework within which you can test decisions, accomplish tasks, and interact with others.

Values help organizations determine a range of acceptable behaviors, defining for leaders and employees alike which actions are encouraged and which are unacceptable. Values tell staff what is good for the organization and what is unhealthy. For example, in our own organization we have defined "receptivity to feedback" as a value that is core to our identity. Our collective clarity about this value allows us to more willingly cut ties with contractors or employees who have been unreceptive to feedback even if there are other things we like about them. As a result, we are surrounded by people who are not only easier to work with, but who are also committed to improvement and personal growth.

When organizations explicitly define their true values, they provide immediate clarity for decision making. They provide a reference point in the hiring processes, performance reviews, and any disciplinary actions. An organization's values create helpful boundaries that show staff and clients where the organization will go and where it won't go.

We interviewed a senior executive in the financial industry about how values guide her company's decisions. She said that their values have helped them decide which clients to keep and which to let go. When faced with a client who had engaged in extortion and other unethical business practices, the company decided to end their relationship with that client, even though it had been a large and lucrative business opportunity. She felt that letting the client go was positive for her company because it built the trust of their staff and other clients. By holding firm to their values, they showed everyone that they could be trusted to be ethical.

THE IMPORTANCE OF VALUES

Another person we interviewed described how several years ago, after much consideration, she resigned from a high-paying job in her fast-paced and demanding industry. The office she worked in had doubled in size, and management was driving for even more growth.

A few years earlier, the company had brought in a new manager to take charge. On arrival he gathered the staff and informed them that he was going to consider who would "make the cut" as suitable for the company's future. He described staff as "cogs" in the well-oiled machine he intended to create, and he planned to remove any unnecessary parts.

The person we interviewed made the cut, and over the next few years she rose in rank, making more and more money along the way. However, despite having what looked from the outside like the perfect job, she was drained and unfulfilled. She said that the hardest part was showing up day after day to provide an important service for her clients only to be valued by management for her sales figures alone. She quit as a result.

When we spoke with her, she was still in the same industry but working with a different organization. She came to realize that her work satisfaction was intimately tied to her ability to express who she was through her commitment to her clients and the precision in her work. Living her values *first* was more fulfilling than trying to fit her values into a company's financial goals.

A good part of people's well-being at work comes from their ability to act in ways that are congruent with their values. Much like the example above, many people are proficient at and enjoy their tasks, but they are ultimately dissatisfied because their personal values do not align with those of their employer. On the other hand, when an employee's values are in line with their organization's values, they may do tasks that aren't always enjoyable, but they can still be satisfied.

Just as it is important to be able to identify with an organization's purpose, it is also important to align with its values. Organizations that authentically define their values show employees how to align their behaviors with the things that matter to the organization. They also make it clear where individuals may be out of step with the organization, providing them with an impetus to leave. In either case, defining and communicating values creates clarity for action.

WHO ARE YOUR VALUES FOR?

We believe that an organization's values are most significant to the people who work *within* the organization. At ACHIEVE, we have chosen not to post our values on our website or in public spaces in our office. We didn't write our values with marketing in mind, instead we wrote them for *us* as a tool for guiding and protecting our culture. Because we prefer for our values to be evident in our actions, we were reluctant to include them in this book, but we felt an example would be helpful. They can be found on page 33.

If you plan to publicize your values, consider what your goals are in doing so. If your intent is to let your clients or customers know the standard to which they can hold you accountable, write that as a separate list. It should certainly be congruent with your values, but it doesn't need to be written in the same way. Values are for your people, while customer or client service standards are for those you serve.

HOW TO DEFINE ORGANIZATIONAL VALUES

We find Patrick Lencioni's book *The Advantage* particularly insightful, and much of what we write here is inspired by his ideas.[4]

In our work with clients around defining values, we focus on the following two categories:

- **DNA values:** Values that make an organization fundamentally unique.
- **Target values:** Values that an organization wishes were true, but they are still working to achieve.

At the heart of every organization lies its *DNA values*. When an organization understands its DNA values, it knows without a doubt what actions and behaviors make it unique in the world. These values define what the organization is like. They provide clarity for decision making and action. They show the organization and the individuals in it *how* they should do what they do in pursuit of their purpose.

The problem is that some organizations only have a vague understanding of what their DNA values actually are. They instead often define their values by what they think they *ought* to be like, what they believe their customers want to see in them, or how they want to be seen – which are really their target values. This frequently results in a long list of values that are difficult to remember and fail to provide useful guidance to employees.

Writing value statements in this way inevitably leads to an uninformative list that is about as interesting as pasta without sauce. Consider values like "customer-service focused," "integrity," and "excellence." Have you ever seen values like these proudly posted on an organization's walls? We certainly have. When we see them, we ask ourselves, "Where's the sauce?"

Values words or phrases like "customer-service focused," "integrity," and "excellence" mean very little without context. These are the sorts of values that any reader would assume your organization would and should have. Posting assumed values is akin to promising "to tell the truth," which might imply that you haven't done that in the past. We usually assume people are telling the truth, and they shouldn't have to assert it. Generic values are the same – you shouldn't have to state them in the first place.

When an organization wants to articulate its DNA values, it must look beyond what anyone would assume to be true and instead search for what makes it distinctive from others that provide the same or similar services. This search must be grounded in behaviors – the positive behaviors that are most valued by the people within the organization.

Try using the following questions as you work to identify your DNA values. When working to develop value statements, be sure to keep them succinct. As you answer these questions, don't worry about how the answers would sound in an advertisement or on your website – this is not an exercise in marketing!

- When your organization is at its best, what behaviors do you see?
- Which behaviors are so important that you would ask an employee to leave if they didn't live them out?

- Which behaviors are so important that you wouldn't apologize for them even if a potential client or customer didn't like them?

At ACHIEVE, we have learned that the answers to these questions are normally gritty and unpolished to begin with. This is okay – and even desirable. Searching for DNA values is like a quest for truth. The quest for truth means discarding polish in favor of raw material, and you often have to dig deep to mine for it. Organizations need to express themselves in ways that are fundamentally true, which means choosing language based on accuracy, not marketing potential.

As we worked to define our values, staff kept saying things like, "We live our workshop content." A phrase like this certainly wouldn't mean much to someone outside of our organization, but *we* knew what it meant. Eventually someone said, "We practice what we teach," and that stuck for us. Now, when we want to describe that DNA value in short-hand, we use the word "embody." This value means a great deal to us – so much so that we hire for its presence and would fire for its absence.

In the pursuit of your DNA values, watch out for "target values." Target values are those that you wish were true of your organization, but which may not be true yet. For instance, we recently worked with a not-for-profit organization that said one of their DNA values was "Everybody is welcome." However, when we asked them who might not feel welcome, the group easily came up with several demographics who weren't represented in the people they served.

They realized in answering our question that "Everybody is welcome" was actually a target value and not yet fully realized. They decided that they needed to do further work in order to make their space more welcoming to several unrepresented groups. They kept "Everybody is welcome" as a target value in recognition that they would need to put effort into making it a reality.

When helping organizations crystalize their DNA and target values, we ask them to pay attention as well to values that show up unintentionally and may be undesirable. In the process of clarifying their values, some organizations look at themselves and discover that all their staff have a university degree or are from one ethnic or cultural background. Embodied traits like these suggest that these organizations might unintentionally value certain demographics over others. Such values should be named and assessed, and they should often be replaced with target values.

A PROCESS FOR DEFINING VALUES

The act of defining values requires leadership to be thoughtful about facilitating conversations and inviting participation from a broad cross section of people connected to the organization. For value statements to be meaningful, they need to resonate with everyone in the organization. The following four steps will help you begin to identify your organizational values:

1. **Create a working group to lead the conversation.** If your organization has fewer than 20 people, include everyone in the discussion of values. For organizations with more than 20 people, a smaller group comprised of leaders and employees from a cross section of the workforce should initially meet to lay the groundwork. This group's goal should be to arrive at a set of values that *may* be true, which can then be tested with others throughout the organization.

2. **Consult with all other leaders, employees, and stakeholders.** When people are consulted during the process, they are more likely to buy into the results. Depending on the size of your organization, you can garner participation through direct discussions, focus groups, and surveys. Listen closely for the stories people tell about your organization. Pay particular attention to the stories of when your organization has been at its best, when its people have rallied together, or when it has stood its ground in spite of a threat. These types of stories illustrate deep values at play.

3. **Synthesize the results.** After others have had a chance to contribute to the conversation, the focus group should meet again to

consider what they have learned through consultation. The group should then refine their initial ideas, but they must avoid the temptation to use generic values language. Instead they should work at expressing values in ways that are unique to the organization. In addition to using single words, values may be expressed in short phrases that insiders will understand or find helpful. Through this process, record behaviors that illustrate the values.

4. **Focus on communication and application.** Once DNA values have been articulated, they must be communicated throughout the organization and reinforced through action. Ensure that it is clear how the values you have written down are acted out within the organization. Encourage individuals and teams to anchor their day-to-day work in the values of the organization. Let people know that these values should be given expression every day and form the basis upon which the organization and those within it will be evaluated. Remember that if these DNA values are not lived out in practical ways every day, employees will develop cynicism about their leaders and the organization's values.

When this process is well facilitated, everyone within your organization should be able to resonate with what one person wrote in response to our survey: "Our values are followed and accepted by everyone in the organization. We talk about them all the time and ensure we are in line with them in every decision we make."

ACHIEVE's DNA Values

We initially went through the process of defining our DNA values a few years ago. However, we recently revisited them with our staff because we felt it was important to make sure they still resonated deeply for all of us. When taken together, the five values listed here describe to our leadership and staff how we should behave. We tried to wrestle the list down to three or four for simplicity, but in the end we all agreed that we needed each of these values in order to remain true to who we are. Some of the individual words may seem like obvious values, but as we defined them in our context, we realized that they were vital to us.

EMBODY – We practice what we teach.
We teach others about respectfulness, effective communication, and conflict resolution. All of us should have the attitudes and abilities to be respectful, to communicate appropriately, and to manage conflict as it comes up.

ENGAGED – We care about our mission and each other.
We care about what we do and why we do it. Our purpose, values, and culture resonate deeply for us. We like our workplace and look forward to connecting with each other and our clients.

FLEXIBLE – We pitch in where needed.
We reject the "that's not in my job description" mentality. We are willing to help each other out on any task because we know everything we do helps us with our mission.

PRODUCTIVE – We get things done individually and collaboratively.
We work quickly and efficiently. We are a small organization accomplishing great things, and that means each of us needs to get things done on our own and within teams.

RECEPTIVE – We are open to feedback and improvement.
We want to get better at what we do, so we strive to respond to feedback in a non-defensive manner. We receive feedback and integrate the content of the feedback promptly.

START HERE

Purpose and values live and breathe together, creating and shaping workplace culture. Together, they allow individuals and teams to align themselves with their organization as a whole, and they provide reference points for dealing with incongruence. (A user-friendly guide for helping you consider purpose and values can be found in the Purpose and Values Questionnaire on page 208 in the Resources section.)

Purpose and values are part of what makes work meaningful. As you clearly articulate the purpose and values that drive the culture of your organization, you will find that you more deeply connect with the people you want to engage. This process sharpens your focus and more clearly shows the people around you why they should engage with your organization in particular.

For those of us who lead organizations, defining and communicating purpose and values is among the most vital work we can do for our organizations. Everything else we do to build a healthy organizational culture starts here.

QUESTIONS FOR REFLECTION

1. To what extent does your organization communicate its purpose? Do you give enough attention to aligning team and individual purpose with organizational purpose?
2. How well do all employees understand the purpose of your organization? If they do not understand your purpose, how could you communicate it more clearly?
3. How much do you think your organization would be missed by staff and clients if it ceased to exist?
4. How involved have staff been in either articulating or discussing your organization's values? In what other ways might you include them in the discussion?
5. What are your organization's DNA and target values? How has your organization used its values to anchor its decisions and actions?

Provide Meaningful Work

WHY WORK?

Why do you work? Why does anyone work? Ask your friends and coworkers, and you are likely to get a variety of answers. But sooner or later, most people will say something along the lines of, "To pay the bills."

Let's begin by acknowledging that most of us do not, and could not, work for free. However, once we have obtained fair and equitable pay, we must ask ourselves: What motivates us to engage with our work at a higher level? Why do some people love their work while others take no pleasure in their tasks? What are the factors that lead to satisfaction at work, and what are some concrete steps we can take to make work meaningful for everyone in our organization? This chapter considers such questions as important factors in creating a workplace culture where people are happily engaged with their work.

In the qualitative responses to our survey, we found that employees had powerful words about their need for meaningful work. One person wrote, "I do mindless, repetitive work that feels like a straitjacket. I need to move on." Another wrote, "We are overly focused on paperwork to the point where *paper* has become more important than the clients we serve." What tragic commentary!

Leaders often bemoan the fact that employees are disengaged. It's true that many people are bored at work. They seem to be passionless and lack interest, not bothering to invest energy in their tasks. Unfortunately, some organizations resort to quick and generic incentives in their effort to improve employee motivation rather than working to provide satisfying and meaningful work that leads to long-term engagement.

If you do a quick online search for "creative ways to engage employees," among the results you'll find suggestions like providing cupcakes, bringing pets to work, and setting up a reward system where employees can redeem points for things like flowers, gift cards, or appliances. These ideas are nice, but they are not necessarily sustainable – after all, who wants or needs a cupcake every single day? The problem with these suggestions is that they fail to get at the root of employee disengagement.

We have learned that the best way to engage employees over the long term is to capitalize on their abilities and provide them with tasks they find rewarding, stimulating, and worthwhile. We define "meaningful work" as work that is purposeful and brings satisfaction to employees by drawing on both their abilities *and* their interests. Meaningful work occurs when purpose aligns with an employee's interests and abilities (see Figure 3.1).

We begin this chapter by looking at why work has such a bad reputation. We then consider how, beginning with hiring practices, leaders can connect the uniqueness of each person to work that is meaningful for them. From there we explore factors that can influence motivation and resistance before finally offering concrete strategies for creating meaning in the work environment.

Where to Find Meaningful Work

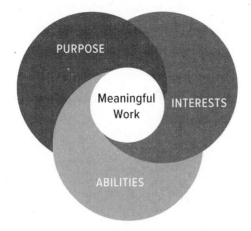

Figure 3.1

WORK'S BAD REPUTATION

If you look up the word "work" in a thesaurus, words like "toil," "slog," "drudgery," and "grind" will be at the top of the list. As a child, I, Wendy, watched my dad work long hours on the farm. He never complained, but from my vantage point, the world of adulthood wasn't one I was eager to enter. Riding my horse across the prairies for hours, wandering in the bush, and swimming in the creek made for a much better life.

It seems that some of us view our work as a necessary evil, not something we'd choose to do if we had an option. Consider the popularity of Tim Ferriss' book *The 4-Hour Workweek*. When I first saw this book, I had an instant negative reaction to the title. It seems to imply that those of us who work more than four hours a week are missing out on the good life. Apparently, less work equals more happiness. But I don't find this to be true at all. Work does not have to be punishment.

Since my early days on the farm, I have grown up to find work that I love! In fact, there would be a hole in my life without it. I don't find my work to be drudgery. I don't necessarily like every aspect of my job, and there are tasks I would rather not have to do, but in the bigger picture, my work brings me immense satisfaction because it is meaningful.

In this chapter, we do not claim to know how to make work meaningful for every person. We do, however, have some clear ideas about what makes work meaningful for most people.

Busyness: The Good & the Bad

Most of us like to have enough to do to keep us from being bored. In fact, many people are at their best when they are busy. In the written portion of our survey, some participants wrote that busyness is part of what makes their work great:

> "My workplace is a very busy atmosphere that challenges me daily."
> "I love the work. It is busy and fast paced."

Others, however, made it clear that being *too* busy can be damaging. These are some factors making their workplaces difficult to like:

> "I have too many competing demands."
> "I don't have enough time to get things done."
> "My workload is so heavy that I work all the time — even at home and on the weekends."

Participants told us that being excessively busy impacts their ability to be effective at work:

> "There isn't the time to keep everyone as informed as they should be."
> "I rarely have the time to learn new things as well as I'd like."
> "There is no time to be proactive. I'm always dealing with day-to-day stuff."

Some participants described the impact on themselves personally:

"I feel exhausted on my days off."

"I always feel inadequate."

"It is demoralizing to go home and worry whose basic needs were missed today because there is not enough of me to go around."

These survey responses should remind us to pay attention to employees' workloads. We should be conscious of how stressed they feel about their work and listen to find out whether busyness is invigorating or damaging for them. When we create environments in which people have the time and resources to delve deeply into what they do, they can be busy and do good work without burning out.

HIRE FOR TALENT & APTITUDE

At ACHIEVE, we have discovered that ensuring employees find meaning in their work begins at the point of first contact: during the interview process. We have dramatically changed our hiring processes over the years. Through trial and error, and observations in our own personal journeys, we have come to appreciate that a person's innate talent matters more than their skill set in determining their satisfaction and effectiveness on the job. Work that connects someone's natural strengths with what they care about allows them to find meaning in the work they do.

Early in our organization's history, we interviewed in the same way that many organizations do – with the goal of finding the most skilled, educated, and experienced candidate. Using this approach worked for us *some* of the time, but the results were unpredictable. We learned that this type of hiring process sometimes gave us employees who were technically capable of doing their jobs, but who found their work unsatisfying or did not resonate with the mission of our company.

As a result, we began to tailor our interviews with the goal of discovering each candidate's innate talent or aptitude while discerning their fit for our culture. It's not that skills, education, and proven experience don't matter, but once those basic requirements are met, they become secondary to a candidate's natural talent and fit.

After shifting the approach of our interviews to assess for innate talent and aptitude, we found that we were much more likely to establish mutually satisfying employment relationships. Innate talent and aptitude helped us determine which candidate would be congruent with the work we needed done.

One of the key questions we ask in interviews is, "What do you do in your current work that gives you a sense of satisfaction?" The answers to this question and others like it tell us what's important to each candidate and whether they would be a fit for the position. (For a list of potential questions, see our Sample Interview Questions on page 209 in the Resources section.)

We recently had an opening in our marketing department. The successful candidate for this position would primarily work independently and not engage with the public. When we asked a very skilled candidate what in his current work gave him satisfaction, his response was, "I love public speaking and being in front of people, sharing ideas." While this person had all the required skills for the job, it was clear that he would not have been satisfied in his work given his desire to work with the public. Partially as a result of this, we didn't hire him.

Most of us have likely had jobs that didn't bring us happiness, or we have worked for organizations whose purpose didn't resonate with us. Early in my career, I, Eric, lucked into work that suited me: teaching conflict resolution. I was working as a mediator for a community organization when our training coordinator had to unexpectedly leave his position. I was asked to step in, and by the age of 25, I was teaching groups of adults how to mediate. I loved it! It drew on my natural abilities to organize things, to discuss subjects I was passionate about, to teach, and to help others work through conflict.

When I moved to a new city a few years later, I applied for a job in collaborative labor relations. My mediation and training background seemed to make me a great fit for the position – and to some extent, I was. I had skills that transferred from one industry to another. However, I soon realized that I wasn't entirely happy in my new job. Although I had the right skills, I found that moving from a facilitative role to an advocacy role required a different way of being and thinking.

Over the years I became increasingly uncomfortable and unhappy. So when I had the opportunity to get back into facilitation and training, I jumped at the chance. Now, at ACHIEVE, I get to provide leadership in the field I am passionate about. Once again, I am happy at work and have a great sense of gratification in the work I do. Though it might seem obvious, I've now come to realize that even meaningful work must be personally satisfying if it is to bring happiness over the long term.

IDENTIFY WHAT PEOPLE LIKE TO DO

If they are to find their work meaningful, a good portion of a person's job should be congruent with the ways in which they think and act. Employees in client services positions should find gratification in helping people. Employees in data management should likewise find pleasure in the accuracy and orderliness required for their jobs. When a new employee's friends can say, "That job sounds like a natural fit for you," they are more likely to find the job meaningful.

The best way for leaders to help employees be successful at work is to find out how they think, why they act in certain ways, and what makes them happy or unhappy, and then help them recognize these traits in themselves. It's important to note that it is rarely possible to find a job in which *every* aspect of work is meaningful, but it is possible for nearly every job to have *some* elements that are.

As leaders, we must go beyond external motivators to encourage our employees to take ownership of their work. Our first step is to identify what motivates them. What do they find pleasure in doing? What sort of work is agreeable to them? Our aim should be to fan the flame of each employee's own motivation.

In addition to aligning with the purpose of the organization, if employees are to find their work personally meaningful, their actual tasks need to be gratifying in and of themselves. It's important to note that the goal is to find a good fit between the organization's needs and the employee's preferences – not simply to let everybody do whatever they want to do.

We recently asked a relatively new employee how she was feeling about her job. She replied: "I love it. I had never considered doing anything like this before, but my friends tell me it makes sense that I would like it." This was incredible validation for our hiring process. She began working on a variety of projects, which included structuring data management processes. In her new role, she was able to use her skills and tap into the kind of orderly thinking she was naturally good at. This ultimately fueled her satisfaction and brought her happiness at work.

This example demonstrates that we should be asking our staff what they find enjoyable and gratifying. When we give our employees tasks that they find rewarding, we allow them to tap into their intrinsic motivation. As a result, we don't have to use rewards or punishments to motivate and engage people.

Once a new employee has been working for a while, ensure that you continue to give them work that brings them satisfaction. This doesn't have to be a mysterious or particularly intuitive process. Instead, you can ask fairly specific and direct questions like these to prompt a dialogue:

- "What parts of your work make you happy?"
- "What daily tasks bring you satisfaction?"
- "Does your work draw on your strengths? If not, how could it?"
- "How do you find the balance between your more satisfying tasks and those you find unpleasant?"

When you have these conversations, listen for excitement in people's voices. Be on the lookout for signs of increased animation in their body language, such as leaning in and smiling. If you keep probing, you just might find areas of untapped potential.

Look for Hidden Talents

Even though we now have a very effective interview process at ACHIEVE, we have been amazed over the years at how often, within several weeks of hiring a new person, we have observed unique and hidden talents that had not shown up on their résumé or during their interview. Sometimes these hidden but valuable talents had not even been known to the employees themselves.

When new projects come up, we take stock of which staff members could do the new tasks best — not based on seniority or job description, but on talent. We ask, "Who on staff is likely to be a natural fit for this task?" Through this process, we begin to test out our employees' talents in ways that they or we did not necessarily envision when we hired them. Often, this process fundamentally changes their role in our organization. We have many stories of employees who started working with us in one capacity before slowly — or sometimes quickly — moving into a completely different role.

For example, one of our employees was hired for a client services position. After a time, she began putting her graphic design skills to use on some projects. She then connected her passion for video to various projects. Eventually, she was so busy with projects that matched her natural talents and passions that, even though she was good at client services, we hired someone else to fill that role. She had become very valuable for us in new ways, and she loved her new role even more than the one we had hired her for.

DISCOVER EACH PERSON'S WORK STYLE

We need to be alert to more than simply what employees enjoy doing or would like to do. Each person brings their own unique work style with them to the workplace. When we understand someone's work style, we can communicate with them more effectively and draw on their natural strengths to help them give their best. Many readily available personality inventories can be used for this purpose, but for our use, we have developed the "ACHIEVE Personality Dimensions Assessment."[1]

This tool identifies four distinct work styles: the "Head," the "Heart," the "Gut," and the "Feet." Although each person expresses themselves in their own unique way, most have a dominant style. Many people also have a strong secondary style as well as a style that they least prefer to use. Each person's style-based strengths reflect who they are at their core and allow them to express the best of who they are. When leaders and their team members learn to understand each other's work styles, they can more easily draw on each other's strengths and work more effectively together.

Here is a quick summary of the four styles:

- **The Head is an analytical work style.** Numbers, facts, and details interest Head people. They tend to be objective, prioritizing proficiency and effectiveness over emotions and opinions. If an individual is precise, exact, and efficient in their work, they might have the Head work style.
- **The Heart is a harmonizing work style.** Those with this style tend to put people, collaboration, and inclusion highest on their priority list. If someone quickly sees the personal and emotional implications of decisions, they might have the Heart work style.
- **The Gut is an intuitive work style.** Someone with a Gut work style is highly intuitive and relies on their *sense* of things. They envision future possibilities and are always wanting to try new strategies and ideas. People with this style often think about what is possible rather than what has already been done.
- **The Feet is a practical work style.** Someone who enjoys concrete and action-based work, and gets bored with those who only seem to *think* and never *do*, might have the Feet work style. Common sense and hands-on problem solving come easily to them.

Just as a body needs a head, a heart, a gut, and feet to function, organizations work best when they have a balance of people with all four styles. As leaders, once we have identified the work style profile of an individual, we are better able to understand the ways in which they like to approach their work. We can more readily assess what comes naturally to them and work to provide them with appropriate tasks.

In our experience, we've found that Head people don't mind analyzing data – a job that is tedious for Heart people, who provide excellent customer service and do great clinical work. Gut people are some of our best innovators, and Feet people get our manuals and marketing materials into the hands of the public.

Of course, this is an oversimplification. That's why it's important to also think about people's secondary and even tertiary styles. For example, even though being a therapist requires Heart energy, it also requires Head energy. The Heart allows people to connect with clients, and the Head allows them to objectively analyze what is going on.

While each person is complex, knowing their primary work style can help us understand how they operate in the world and determine what roles they might find invigorating. As we learn to recognize individual styles, we can also work to create a balance of styles on our teams. Tapping into the style-based strengths of each employee should be a primary goal of every organization.

We are all motivated by getting better at work we enjoy. And when we align people's tasks with their style-based strengths, they are both motivated by their growing sense of mastery and quickly become more proficient and fulfilled in their work.

ONE MORE TIME

Motivation and employee engagement are on the minds of many leaders we meet. However, we rarely hear leaders make the connection between motivation and *meaningful work*. As one of the key ingredients of employee engagement, fulfilling work greatly increases workplace motivation. When an employee's work is meaningful, they will be motivated to challenge themselves and excel at it.

Research over the past several decades has identified some common factors that lead people to experience their work as motivating, regardless of their field. Frederick Herzberg describes these factors in a classic article titled "One More Time: How Do You Motivate Employees?" He explains that "achievement, recognition for achievement, the work itself, responsibility, and growth or advancement" are all primary motivators in the workplace.[2]

In his book *Drive*, Daniel H. Pink similarly explains that "the ingredients of genuine motivation ... [are] autonomy, mastery, and purpose."[3] Herzberg's article was first published in 1968, Pink's book came out in 2009, and here we are again, years later, addressing motivation and meaning *one more time.* It seems that management practices are slow to change, and not all leaders have been willing to learn from research and past mistakes. We may be eager to hear new ideas, but some organizations are slow to act on what is known to be true about motivation. In reality, after years of research, not much has changed when it comes to how best to engage employees.

WHOSE MOTIVATION ARE WE TALKING ABOUT?

One of the problems with motivation is that we often don't consider *who* actually wants the work to be done. It is typically a leader who wants work done in a particular way or within a precise time frame. It is *their* motivation that is the impetus for action. Many leaders provide negative or positive reinforcement in an effort to motivate employees to accomplish required work in their preferred manner. In these cases, it is *not* the employee's own motivation that primarily initiates and drives the work.

Recently, I, Wendy, was struggling to convince my son to clean his room. After several unsuccessful reminders, I issued some negative reinforcement in the form of a potential punishment: "Clean your room or I'll take your phone away." In this scenario, I was the one who was highly motivated for his room to be clean. My threat of negative reinforcement did work, and my son reluctantly cleaned his room, but a week later it was back to its original disheveled state, and he was in no way disturbed by its return to chaos.

Learning from my mistake, I thought I'd offer some positive reinforcement instead, in the form of a bribe: "If you clean your room, I'll give you some extra money for your weekend plans." Again, it worked, and he cleaned his room. But a week later – you guessed it – the room was a mess. This time when I reminded him to clean it up, he asked me what I would give him in return!

In our attempts to motivate actions, we often resort to what Herzberg calls KITA (Kick In The Ass) motivators. These types of motivators can be either positive or negative reinforcements, as in the examples above. They typically sound something like, "Do this or else" (negative) or, "Do this and you will get something in return" (positive). Though these motivators may lead to desired outcomes, the results are often short-lived and unsustainable, even leading to negative consequences in the long run. Unfortunately, KITA motivators are still widely used by parents, schools, and businesses.

In his book *The Best Place to Work*, Ron Friedman explains that "it's [the] feeling of personal ownership that inspires employees to be driven by their own interests, curiosity, and desires to succeed."[4] The reality is that we, as leaders, cannot motivate our employees. Ultimately, we need to recognize that long-term motivation comes from within.

Instead of trying to motivate employees, your task as a leader is to find out what *already* motivates them. This is a subtle but profound shift. It's not *what you do to your employees* that will engage them, but rather the opportunities for fulfillment you provide them with that will ultimately tap into *their* motivation for doing their best work. Pay attention to what is important to them – it is *their* motivation you are aiming to stimulate.

Returning to the story of my son's mess, my third attempt at motivating him was more successful. We sat down and had a conversation. I asked him why he wasn't cleaning his room, and why the mess didn't bother him. He responded by telling me that his room wasn't his favorite place to be. For context, a few months earlier, his sister had left for university, and we had moved my son into her now empty room. Though he had long outgrown his old bedroom, it turned out that he hadn't settled into the new space. He didn't like the color or décor, and it felt stark to him.

Together, we planned some changes. We took a few trips to IKEA, set up his electric piano in the corner, and put up several basketball posters. These adjustments – along with a very big laundry hamper – were all it took to make the room feel right to him. He quickly took pride in his new space, and he began to keep it clean.

Providing KITA motivators for work can have unanticipated consequences. When you reward people with incentives beyond their salary, the incentives often become an expectation. And if you decide to remove the reward, it may be perceived as a punishment. This past year, we've had conversations with several clients who have asked about the value of incentives for their employees. One leader we spoke with stated that the employee incentive program they had implemented was having the opposite effect they had hoped for. Employees had become unwilling to help their coworkers and were not willing to go above and beyond unless they had an additional incentive.

A LESSON FROM *I LOVE LUCY*

In a memorable scene from *I Love Lucy*, Lucy and her coworker Ethel – who find themselves working in a chocolate factory – are informed that they are responsible for wrapping each candy that passes by them on a conveyor belt. They are told that if one candy gets by without a wrapper, they will be fired. The candies keep coming faster and faster, so Lucy and Ethel begin to gobble them up in hopes of meeting their supervisor's expectations and getting their paychecks.[5] Though this is a comical example, a similar thing can also happen in our workplaces – when our motivation systems are only based on punishments, they may end up producing the wrong behavior.

DON'T MAKE THEM DO IT

As leaders, we tend to like processes that are *lean, streamlined, efficient,* and *practical.* These words are used in our conversations all the time, and they are the mantras of many organizations. But employees are not processes or procedures, they are human beings. And humans don't typically respond well to having their lives fixed or streamlined, especially when they feel handled, coerced, or manipulated.

I, Michael, once had a friend who was in the habit of asking me for advice about his problems at work. He would describe a problem and then present me with his two options: one that I recognized as a "foolish" path and another that seemed to be the "wise" path.

After offering my advice a number of times, I realized that whenever I suggested the wise path, he chose the foolish path. I was intrigued by this, so I decided to try an alternative approach. I started suggesting the foolish path, and sure enough, he started to take the wise path instead!

Psychologists refer to this phenomenon as "reactance." When people feel that their options are being limited, they tend to push back against those perceived limitations. Think about a young child who is told *not* to touch something – more often than not, they touch it immediately. Or think back to when you were a teenager – when you were told you *had* to do something, you likely dragged your feet or mumbled under your breath.

Young children and teenagers are not the only ones who respond with reactance – adults do as well. When we try to make employees do things *our* way – when we limit their autonomy – they often start to feel micromanaged or feel the need to defend themselves. They may even purposely deliver inferior work. Over time employees may become apathetic, stop making decisions for themselves, and become dependent on their supervisors for constant direction.

Everyone – from CEOs to entry-level employees – wants to feel like they are given a level of independence to make their own decisions. If leaders require their employees to check in regarding every decision, their employees will soon become apathetic and grow dependent on the constant input from their managers. This dependent state is the antithesis of a thriving culture where people find meaning in their work.

DEALING WITH RESISTANCE TO DIRECTION

Everyone is occasionally resistant to direction. Sometimes the resistance is on the surface, and an employee tells us they disagree or don't want to do what we are asking. At other times, it is covert – the employee drags their feet, procrastinates, or complains to others.

When employees are resistant to direction, either openly or covertly, there is often a simple solution: give them more autonomy. The more independence we give people, the less they tend to resist. Here are five tips for dealing with employees who tend to resist direction:

- Begin by asking them what *they* think should be done.
- If their solution isn't ideal, but it is still sufficient, let them proceed their way. Their buy-in is usually worth it.
- If their solution is not a viable option, explain why you think so and lay out some options you *can* live with.
- If 90 percent of your message is that they must do exactly as you say, emphasize the 10 percent where they do have a choice.
- Even when you feel that the way forward is obvious, always ask what *they* think first. Most of the time, they will give you the obvious answer but feel they came upon the solution themselves.

When employees have autonomy – when they're not simply told what to do – they normally work harder, are more creative, and are willing to persist longer.

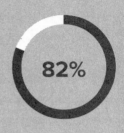

I have autonomy in how I do my work.

According to our survey, 82 percent of people who like their workplace also have autonomy in how they do their work.

82%

PRACTICAL WAYS TO MAKE WORK MEANINGFUL

So far in this chapter, we have considered why meaningful work matters, what motivates people, and how people work in different ways. The rest of this chapter focuses on practical and simple strategies for making work more meaningful.

Push Boundaries

Most people want to do work that stimulates and challenges them. In our organization, we have learned that employees are more likely to be engaged and thrive when their boundaries are pushed slightly beyond what they think they can do. We have seen firsthand how employees will rise to the challenge of working on projects that are new to them or tasks that require them to use hidden talents or develop new skills.

Our employees have sometimes been surprised by the level of responsibility and trust we give them. The more important and challenging the work entrusted to them, the more encouraged and validated they feel by us as management. They also have the pleasure of working on a variety of new tasks.

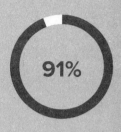

The work I do challenges me in a positive way.

According to our survey, 91 percent of people who like their workplace also have work that challenges them in a positive way.

Focus on Job Enrichment, Not More Work

In an attempt to make work more challenging, managers may sometimes ask for higher outputs of an employee's tasks. For example, if an employee easily meets their requirement of producing 10 "widgets" per hour and approaches their manager asking for more challenge, the manager might increase the goal to 15. While increasing productivity requirements does increase the challenge of work, it usually isn't the right kind of challenge and will normally lead to less satisfaction, not more.

Rather than simply adding more duties in an effort to stimulate employees, leaders should rather strive to provide opportunities for people to move more deeply into what brings them satisfaction. For instance, if an employee finds satisfaction in interacting with customers – and this is a valuable role in the organization – leaders should find ways to increase their contact with customers.

Remove Useless Tasks

Removing useless tasks may seem like an obvious priority, but if you examine the various responsibilities of people on your team, you may find that some of their tasks are of little or no organizational value. We find it important to ask questions like these to ensure people aren't doing useless tasks:

- How many emails are copied to and read by people who don't need the information?
- How many employees write reports that no one reads?
- How much data is tracked but never used?
- How many documents do people print that are already stored electronically?
- How often are you asked questions regarding information that could easily be found by the person asking the question?
- How often are you asked for direction by employees who are capable of setting their own direction?

From time to time, it's important to take stock of tasks and eliminate some of them. The worst use of time is doing something that doesn't need to be done in the first place.

Give Complete Units of Work

Most people find it satisfying to finish things, to check items off their lists, and to be able to look back and say, "I did that!" Knowing this, leaders should find ways to assign complete units of work whenever possible, allowing employees to see tasks through from beginning to end and experience a sense of completion. For example, it is beneficial to have the employee who helped write a report participate in presenting it to management. This not only increases their sense of responsibility, it also provides a sense of satisfaction in completing a task.

The reality is that many of the tasks within an organization are small contributions to a much larger final product. In these situations, it's important that employees are able to experience the end product in some way. For example, share stories of customer satisfaction with your team, share project results with everyone who participated, and acknowledge people's contributions.

Provide Support and Resources

As leaders, we need to ensure that our employees have the training and resources they need to do what we expect of them. Desire and aptitude are not enough for our employees to be happy at work. They need both meaning and challenge in their work, but they also need support to meet these challenges. As employees evolve in their roles, we need to continually respond to their growth.

In order to work with this process, routinely ask your employees questions like these:

- "What do you need in order to do your job well?"
- "Who can you ask if you need help?"
- "How are your processes and procedures working for you?"
- "What are some ways in which your job could be made easier?"

In our organization, these types of questions always result in valuable insights. Some employees tell us they are feeling great about their work. Some are looking for additional challenges and have useful ideas for change, while others are already feeling overwhelmed. With this new information, we can work to bring better balance for everyone.

The key is to actually have these conversations. One survey participant noted, "While I greatly appreciate my autonomy, I often feel isolated and wish my leader would check in with me more often." Let's not assume that employees have found the right balance, or that they don't need our support.

Foster Professional Development

Most people like to learn new things. At ACHIEVE, we encourage our employees to tell us about professional development opportunities they are interested in. We also intentionally plan for each employee's professional development throughout the year. We have always encouraged employees to attend training sessions either in person or online. But we have found that, unless they have a clear plan, most people don't take time for professional development.

Now that we are more intentional about scheduling training, professional development actually happens. As a result, our employees are exposed to new and different ways of thinking. This helps us meet new challenges as well as capitalize on opportunities related to our work.

Make regular professional development a deliberate conversation and expectation within your organization. These discussions around professional development, job satisfaction, and meaningful and challenging work all complement each other.

YOU CAN'T PLEASE EVERYONE

A bit of realism is necessary when we're talking about meaningful work. As in most human endeavors, there are no guarantees. It is faulty reasoning to think that just because we follow a list of strategies – even the ones outlined in this book – we will be assured satisfaction and productivity. We can engage in culture-creating activities, structure roles, and provide meaningful and challenging work, but we may still have employees who are not satisfied.

In his book *Flow*, Mihaly Csikszentmihalyi describes *flow* as an ideal phenomenon in which one's attention is fully absorbed in the experience at hand. To reach this state, two factors are necessary: First, the work needs to be goal defined and challenging while offering immediate feedback. Second, the person's personality must allow them to achieve a state of flow. If a person's personality prevents them from achieving flow, they "will be discontented even with a potentially great job."[6]

There is a small segment of people who do not want more responsibility – they do not want more challenging work. There are some employees who will never strive to do more than simply keep their job.

We have little control over self-limiting factors such as these, but we do have immense control over the work environments we create, and it is here that we should focus our energy.

YOU CAN PLEASE *ALMOST* EVERYONE

Though we can't please everyone, we *can* please most people with work that is rewarding. When we provide opportunities for satisfying and meaningful work, we create work cultures that tap into potential, inspire loyalty, and draw out the best from everybody.

Employees enter organizations with existing sets of strengths, skills, and knowledge ready to apply within their new workplace settings. The ways in which they are empowered to contribute through their strengths, skills, and knowledge directly affect both their well-being and the workplace cultures around them. If we don't offer meaningful work – work that finds the sweet spot between an employee's interests and abilities and our organization's purpose and needs – our employees will eventually disengage.

Making work meaningful should be a priority for everyone who has the power to influence their workplace. While productivity is crucial to the success of every organization, emphasizing productivity alone takes a significant toll on workplace culture and employee motivation. We as leaders need to have our priorities in order. If we focus first and foremost on making work meaningful for our employees, they will most certainly be more satisfied and productive.

QUESTIONS FOR REFLECTION

1. In what ways does your organization provide meaningful work to employees?

2. How can you adjust your hiring process to look for talent instead of qualification? What are some questions you can ask candidates to determine whether they'll enjoy the position?

3. How can you better align people's tasks with their strengths? What other activities and projects could specific employees be a part of that would bring them satisfaction?

4. What talents do your employees have that are waiting to be tapped into? What do you need to do to find these talents and unleash them?

5. In what circumstances do you tend to rely on KITA motivators, such as punishments or rewards? What are the positive and negative impacts of these motivators in the short and long term?

Focus Your Leadership Team on People

THE LEADERSHIP EFFECT

An organization's CEO may be brilliant, its employees may be great to work with, and the work it does may have a valuable purpose, but if its leaders aren't easy to work for, there's a good chance it won't be a healthy place to work. When we write "easy to work for," we're referring to leaders who are respectful, caring, attentive, and effective as communicators. These are leaders who demonstrate that they care about employees for who they are as people, not just for the work they do. When leaders lack these traits, it is very difficult for employees to be happy at work.

The saying, "People don't quit organizations, they quit their bosses," is well known because it's true. While some employees do not literally quit, they are sure to be less motivated and engaged when their direct supervisors are not easy to respect or like.

Great workplaces have great leaders who focus on people, not merely profit or productivity. This theme has re-emerged many times throughout our own personal experiences, in conversations with our employees and those in other organizations, and in the responses to our survey.

This chapter looks at the specific ways in which leadership impacts workplace culture. We begin by making a case for caring leadership and exploring what that means. We also consider the importance of developing employees, offer advice on how to be a leader worth following, and explore the best ways to provide accountability for your staff. And because we believe that leadership development is a continual process, we conclude with a look at how to develop yourself as a leader.

SURVEY STATISTICS

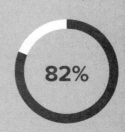

My direct supervisor cares about me as a person.

According to our survey, 82 percent of people who like their workplace also have a supervisor who cares about them.

CARING LEADERSHIP MAKES A DIFFERENCE

One of the easiest things we can do as leaders to increase the morale and effectiveness of employees is to demonstrate that we care about them. As several of our survey participants noted, this can sometimes be as simple as showing interest in what is going on in their lives. One participant wrote, "My supervisor is compassionate and genuinely interested in how I'm doing." Another wrote, "I am cared for as a person, not just as an employee." When we show genuine interest, we demonstrate that we value employees as people, not simply for the products they produce.

One person we interviewed shared her story of working within an unhealthy organizational culture. Her experience was typical of other stories we've heard over the years. In her organization, employees experienced fear on multiple levels. There was a high level of toxic conflict, and leadership was either indifferent or complicit in these negative behaviors. Not surprisingly, productivity was dismal and employee turnover was high.

The part of her story that really jumped out to us was that she had worked with that organization for close to a year, but her direct supervisor still didn't know she had children. To be clear, it is not always appropriate to ask people about the details of their personal lives. However, when we show even moderate interest in people, information about their personal lives inevitably comes up.

On a practical level, knowing whether an employee has children will not automatically increase their performance or the organization's success. But we have learned that when leaders demonstrate interest in employees' lives – when they ask questions about their families, vacations, hobbies, and passions – employees feel more valued, respected, and cared for. In one long-term study, professors of management Sigal G. Barsade and Olivia A. O'Neill found that employees who worked in a loving, caring culture were less likely to burn out, missed fewer days of work, worked more effectively with teams, and had higher levels of job satisfaction.[1] As this research shows, caring about employees is an effective way of creating a healthier and more productive workplace.

'But I'm Not Your Therapist!'

Leaders who are trying to be supportive sometimes ask us, "How can I be a caring leader without becoming my employees' go-to support person when they are going through crises?" In our experience, it's important to remember that there are usually other people and resources in employees' lives that are better positioned to provide support.

From a practical perspective, leaders must balance caring for employees with their other leadership tasks. We have found that what employees usually need most is acknowledgment of the things going on in their lives.

If employees are seeking too much of your time for personal matters, be honest and frank about your limitations while still remaining sensitive to their problems. Offer feedback along these lines:

I'm glad you feel you can come to me with this issue. I see this issue is causing you significant stress. I want to support you through this, but I do have limits on how much time I have available to meet with you about this. I encourage you to seek the support of your friends and family. I will, however, touch base with you from time to time to see how things are going.

You may also be supportive of people's needs by directing them to professionals or other resources within the organization. For example, many organizations offer counseling services through their insurance providers or have designated people to respond to concerns about employee well-being. In addition, there may be community resources to which you can refer employees or other people within your organization who are better positioned to provide support.

THE PROBLEM WITH OLD-SCHOOL MANAGERS

Early in my career, I, Randy, worked for a manager who clearly embodied an "old-school" management style. He was full of bravado and purposely intimidating. He was a terrible listener and would frequently yell in an effort to get his desired results.

Initially, it was exciting to be around him. I felt an intoxicating energy in his presence, and my desire to please him and receive his approval was motivating. However, after a few months, his old-school management style grew, well, *old*! My desire to please him and excel waned. I found myself looking for the "exit door," and I soon found my way out.

When we teach and consult in organizations, people often describe "old-school," "directive," or "traditional" management styles – and they don't use these terms in a good way. In our survey, participants also used words like "sociopath," "autocratic," and "mini-dictator" to describe this type of management.

Most of us have a clear picture of what these terms mean. They refer to management styles where the boss says "Jump," and employees ask, "How high?" They are approaches where yelling, barking orders, and pounding fists (sometimes literally) are considered the best ways to get results. Opinions inconsistent with those of the manager are quickly silenced, for there is only one right way: the manager's way. One of our survey participants gave a good description of this management style: "My manager is a bully who 'chews people up and spits them out.' She regularly engages in verbal and mental abuse." Another person reported: "My immediate supervisor's management style is 'command and control,' and he is not open to suggestions. He has squashed my creativity and made my daily job drudgery."

In our experience, employees in organizations and teams where this style is present either quickly fall in line or look for a way out of the organization. For those who stay, creativity and engagement are replaced with compliance and silent acceptance. Employees learn that it's best to avoid being noticed.

It's important to highlight that this style of management is not practiced only by older leaders. Younger leaders who have grown up under this style of management often use the same approach as those who mentored them. In addition, some industries that use chain-of-command leadership structures may encourage this style of management.

One of the reasons old-school management continues is that many organizations still hire people based on outdated practices. Take a look at some job ads for management positions, and you will often find phrases such as "highly competitive," "independent thinker," and "career fast-track" instead of words like "collaborative," "caring," and "intuitive." The first list emphasizes individualism and competition, which align well with old-school management styles.

The problem with old-school management is that it sacrifices employee satisfaction for short-term results. Sacrificing employee happiness means forgoing long-term performance. Employees who work under old-school managers would certainly not say they have "a great place to work."

'Don't Judge My Bathroom Breaks'

As we were writing this book, we asked several of our staff who had previously expressed that they like working at our organization *why* they like their workplace. They mentioned liking their coworkers and appreciating that leadership involves them in decision making, but the most surprising response was, "I like that I'm not judged for when I go to the bathroom."

After some laughter, we asked for a bit more context. The employee explained that he recently heard of someone who worked in an organization that limited the time and frequency of bathroom breaks.

To him, this type of micromanagement showed a great distrust of employees. In his view, such authoritarian ways would not make a great place to work. He went on to explain that when he compares that type of environment to the one he's currently in — one in which he gets to organize his own day, make decisions about his workflow, and go to the bathroom when he wants to — he is grateful for his workplace.

DIRECTIVE VERSUS EMPOWERING LEADERSHIP

A recent study published by the *Academy of Management Journal* makes a distinction between *empowering* leadership and *directive* leadership. Natalia M. Lorinkova and her coauthors define empowering leadership approaches as those that prioritize "sharing power with subordinates and raising their level of autonomy and responsibility."[2] In addition, empowering leaders promote collaborative decision making, information sharing, and teamwork. Directive leadership, in contrast, uses a leader's positional power to actively structure the work of subordinates and lay out expectations for their compliance.

Empowering leaders trust employees to make meaningful contributions, while directive leaders outline the consequences of not meeting expectations. Empowering leadership is about enabling success, while directive leadership is about preventing failure. The study concludes that:

> Teams led by a directive leader initially outperform those led by an empowering leader. However, despite lower early performance, teams led by an empowering leader experience higher performance improvement over time because of higher levels of team-learning, coordination, empowerment, and mental model development.[3]

Over the long term, directive management approaches are not only less effective, they also move organizations further away from being places where people like to work. In contrast, empowering leaders create workplaces that are full of happier, more engaged, and more productive employees.

SURVEY RESPONSES

Micromanagement & Decision Making

Many of our survey participants identified micromanaging leadership as a factor that prevents their workplace from being great. With obvious frustration about her manager, one participant lamented, "She thinks she is fixing things, but in reality, she is creating a dysfunctional organization."

Although micromanagement might seem like something a manager would do consistently, one participant humorously disparaged their boss as periodically feeling "a sudden need to micromanage."

Participants also complained about leaders who make decisions without consulting staff, making them feel "excluded and powerless." They wrote that these leaders waste time and decrease morale:

"The decisions change the direction of work that is in progress."
"Years of experience and a wealth of knowledge that long-term employees bring to the table are being wasted."
"Opportunities to get some buy-in from the employees are missed."

In our survey, participants so frequently complained about top-down and micromanaging leadership that one could easily wonder whether it is the norm. However, some of our participants described leaders who are different. One raved: "There is *no* element of fear. If either myself or others make a mistake, the leadership takes this as a learning opportunity." Others noted that they appreciate having input into decisions:

"Management encourages ideas and gives authority to staff to follow through on those ideas."
"I feel comfortable speaking up when it's important, and I know my opinion will be valued."
"As part of a team, we have direction in how we will address general problems. Our input and ideas are welcomed."
"We, as employees, are able to express ourselves to the fullest. There is a great deal of trust. At work I feel 'at home.'"

It's clear that people find micromanagement and top-down decision making insulting. It is an approach to leadership that hurts workplace culture by devaluing employees and discounting their abilities. Leaders do well when they give staff a measure of autonomy in completing tasks and value employees' opinions in decision making.

HOW TO BE A LEADER WORTH FOLLOWING

Are you honest and respectful? Do you lead by example? Do you do what you say you will do? Do you take responsibility for your mistakes? If you can't answer these questions with a resounding "Yes," chances are some of the people you are supposed to be leading are not following you.

We define a leader as someone who *inspires* and *influences* others to willingly act – leaders motivate employees to act because they want to, not because they have to. Leaders who are willingly followed have earned *trust* and are therefore able to influence others without using coercion. In organizations with effective leaders, employees willingly take on tasks and go the extra mile – not because they are forced to, but because they want to.

Work on these three core elements of leadership to contribute to a strong workplace culture:

1. **Build trust.** If employees don't trust you, you will never be able to get desired results from them. This is why you must work toward developing relationships of mutual trust. When you care about your employees and have *their* interests in mind, not just the organization's, you increase the amount of confidence they have in you. In fact, the strongest correlation we found in our survey data was the connection between leaders who have established trust and those who have demonstrated that they care. (To learn more about this connection, see page 190 of our Survey Analysis.)

2. **Inspire others.** Employees are inspired by leaders who are genuinely enthusiastic about their organization's mission and vision and who can articulate how their organization makes a difference. To be an inspiring leader, you must be positive, verbalize your enthusiasm for projects, and express gratitude for your team. You should also ensure that everyone feels included in your organization's mission and vision so that it is shared and collective – one that everyone is excited about and proud of.

3. **Exert conscious influence**. As a leader, your voice is amplified – you play a significant role in influencing your team toward its goals. To do this effectively, you need to practice conscious influ-

ence, which means carefully discerning where and when you voice your opinions, ask for advice, and give direction. Remember: respected leaders build their influence through trust and inspiration, not by imposing their authority.

Although much more can be expected of a leader, these three elements are foundational for becoming a leader who is worth following.

DEVELOPING A MENTORING CULTURE

One often-overlooked strategy for creating a culture where people like to work is to consciously and consistently develop employees through mentorship. Investing in staff in this way creates opportunities for meaningful relationships, shows employees that they are valued, and allows them to develop their abilities, which will ultimately help the organization.

A mentoring culture may include formal structures with set times allocated for mentorship. Some organizations use a curriculum or program as part of the learning process. In other organizations, mentoring may take on a less formal structure in which each employee is paired with a more seasoned or knowledgeable coworker who becomes their mentor.

Some organizations make the mistake of only selecting the highest performing employees for mentorship. In our view, this creates the potential for division among employees and may demotivate those who are not chosen. Instead of focusing only on the "top" performers at ACHIEVE, we take the view that everyone should be developed, and most will excel where they have aptitude when they are given the proper support.

One of the key requirements of successful mentoring is availability. Leaders must be available if they are going to help employees succeed. I, Randy, remember going to my manager's office as a young worker to ask for a suggestion on a project only to be met with a "death stare" that asked, "What would possess you to interrupt me?" In that organization, I had seen firsthand how leaders would become upset when employees didn't develop as quickly as desired, yet the leaders were not even willing to make themselves available.

Mentorship-oriented leaders get more effort out of their employees by spending time with them, thinking about them, and caring for them. Mentoring others is about building relationships, and relationships require time. When we spend time mentoring others, it demonstrates to them that we believe in their abilities and, more importantly, that we believe in them as people.

DEVELOPING CHARACTER

It's often said that an organization's people are its most valuable resources. Though it is well understood that a key role of a good leader is helping employees develop their skills, we often overlook the importance of *character* development for both leaders and employees.

We all want to be good at what we do, and it is equally important to be surrounded by competent coworkers. Highly skilled people can do amazing things. But skills are like tools in the hands of a builder – the builder's intentions make all the difference in how they complete the job. A builder can use their tools to construct something well, or they can choose to cut corners to finish a job quickly. In a similar way, a leader who is a highly skilled communicator may choose to present all the information, or they can emphasize only those things that support their view. Character makes all the difference.

People of character are those who live their values in ways that strengthen the communities they're a part of, act selflessly, and are accountable for what they do. When our coworkers and employees have strength of character, we trust them because we know they will make principled decisions in both the good times and the bad.

Character development begins by surrounding ourselves with people whose values and behaviors we trust. When we are surrounded by people of admirable character, we strive to live up to their values. We are also more likely to receive honest and effective feedback when we do make mistakes. In a way, they hold up "mirrors" in which we can see ourselves more clearly, allowing us to consider whether our actions line up with how we wish to be seen.

Just as people have character, so do organizations. The character of an organization is intimately connected to the character of the individuals who work there. If we care about the character of our workplace, we must care about the character of each person we hire. Our candidates should be able to act in ways that are congruent with our stated organizational values.

As leaders at ACHIEVE, we measure our individual and collective actions on a daily basis against the values we have identified as an organization. For instance, we believe that people ought to be treated in ways that *they* find respectful. When facing a dilemma with a client, we first ask ourselves what would be best for the client, not how we can resolve the situation cheaply or efficiently. Ultimately, developing character means developing the capacity to make consistent, values-based decisions, which creates trust both within and outside the organization.

THE 'NO NEWS IS GOOD NEWS' FALLACY

Some managers are like the person who tells their partner, "I said 'I love you' when we first got together, and I'll let you know if anything changes." The underlying belief here is that no news is good news. Despite the fact that, for leaders, no news often *is* good news, some employees fill the silence with worry about whether they are doing the right thing or are appreciated.

Employees want to be valued and appreciated by their leaders. Unfortunately, some managers seem to fear that "excessive" recognition will dilute their praise, cheapen it, and reduce motivation for future outstanding performance. This is simply not true.

In their *HBR* article "The Ideal Praise-to-Criticism Ratio," Jack Zenger and Joseph Folkman write, "Only positive feedback can motivate people to continue doing what they're doing well, and do it with more vigor, determination, and creativity."[4] Drawing on multiple studies, the authors state that the mere acknowledgment of good performance increases the likelihood of good performance in the future. Furthermore, giving *specific* feedback – telling a person exactly *what* you liked and *why* you liked it – dramatically increases the likelihood of that level of performance occurring again.

If employees are going to find value in the work they do each day, they need to hear that their efforts matter – that leaders notice their work and are willing to pause to acknowledge and validate contributions. Without encouragement, people wonder whether they are appreciated and may question whether their contributions matter to the organization's success.

Offering validation is an important strategy for increasing workplace satisfaction and creating a healthy workplace culture. When we see praiseworthy attitudes and actions, we should not keep our observations to ourselves, but instead verbalize our thoughts and offer words of validation and praise.

I, Michael, will never forget working in human resources and having to tell a recent immigrant, who really needed a job, that she had not been the successful candidate. It was difficult for me because I knew how hard it would be for her.

After watching me deliver the bad news, my manager gave me an immediate and affirming response that is still vivid in my mind: "You're going to be a great human resources manager – you handled that with empathy and compassion." By telling me what I had done well, she reinforced the importance of approaching people with sincerity and understanding. Her words gave me the fuel to continue with the often challenging work of human resources.

Recognizing positive behaviors reinforces them. Validation can be as simple as a statement like, "I could see that the way you listened to that client really worked to create a better relationship." People need to know that they are doing things correctly so they can continue doing those things. When validation is done publicly, it reinforces a positive workplace culture across the organization.

It's also important to consider the content of our validations. In his book *The Man Who Lied to His Laptop*, Clifford Nass emphasizes the importance of being specific and creative when giving feedback:

[An] approach for enhancing positive evaluations is surprise because it gets people to pay attention and think harder about what you just said. For example, if you compliment someone on something that he. or she thinks you are unaware of, it will have a bigger effect than if you keep dishing out the same obvious compliments.[5]

When giving feedback, think differently. Don't just state the obvious – describe what is special and unique about the person or their behavior.

CREATING A CULTURE OF ACCOUNTABILITY

Accountability is one of the pillars of a highly functional and healthy workplace culture. Simply put, accountability means that people take responsibility for what they say they will do and what they have already done.

Accountability and trust walk hand in hand. When we do what we say we will do, we establish trust. When an employee commits to completing a project within an atmosphere of accountability, we trust that they will do so. In a culture of accountability, everyone can plan their work accordingly, knowing that others are working to get things done when they say they'll have them done. And when someone lets the team down, they will take responsibility for correcting their mistake.

Like most aspects of organizational culture, creating a culture of accountability starts with leadership. When leaders are willing to be accountable, they set the tone for everyone else. When leaders promise to complete tasks by a particular time and in a particular way, they need to deliver. When leaders make mistakes, or fail to deliver on their commitments, they must take responsibility and work to correct their mistakes. When leaders are willing to be held accountable for their work, they make it easier for others to be held accountable as well.

One of the best ways to ensure accountability within an organization is to be clear about what is going to be done, when, and by whom. Clarity about details creates standards by which results can be measured. Recording details in meeting minutes, and then reviewing those minutes as a team, creates accountability. Publicly sharing goals and providing progress updates increases accountability.

To improve accountability among staff, encourage positive peer influence. When it comes to team performance, the behaviors of individuals are often shaped by what they see others doing. When someone takes responsibility for their part in a project, or even their part in failure, it encourages their peers to do the same. Be sure to highlight ways in which team members rely on each other to be accountable for their commitments.

Mutual accountability and mutual support reinforce each other. In order to create the conditions for positive peer influence, peers need to have healthy relationships with each other. In the absence of healthy relationships, people care less about accountability and more about self-protection. However, in the context of strong relationships, leaders can hold conversations with teams about what their goals are and how they will practice mutual accountability in working toward those goals. Team members can also discuss goals among themselves in ways that are both supportive and appropriately challenging.

One key challenge for leaders is to step back far enough to allow employees to hold each other accountable. If a leader is the only one responsible for accountability conversations, the team is let off the hook, peer accountability suffers, and leaders have to do all the work. In a context of accountability and positive peer influence, a leader's role is to bring conversations back to goals and deadlines when teams become distracted, but not to micromanage accountability.

Healthy and high-performing teams and organizations empower employees to be accountable, resulting in high levels of trust among everyone in the organization. Cultures of accountability create the conditions for increased productivity and higher quality work.

FOUR APPROACHES TO ACCOUNTABILITY

Organizations can approach accountability in four distinct ways, as we explain with a model called the Accountability Grid (see Figure 4.1). We've adapted this matrix from Ted Wachtel's use of the Social Discipline

Window, a conflict resolution tool.[6] The four approaches are based on varying levels of both accountability and support:

- **Ignoring:** Avoiding problems we'd like to see fixed (low accountability, low support).
- **Enabling:** Supporting employees while excusing their unhealthy behaviors or failing to consistently address their mistakes (low accountability, high support).
- **Punishing:** Providing accountability through the imposition of disciplinary procedures without supporting long-term change (high accountability, low support).
- **Transforming:** Providing accountability for unhealthy behaviors while offering adequate support for long-term growth (high accountability, high support).

Using the Accountability Grid, we show responses along two axes, which are on a continuum of support from low to high and a continuum of accountability from low to high (see Figure 4.1).

The Accountability Grid

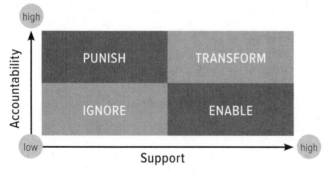

Figure 4.1

When support and accountability are both low, it is typically because leaders are ignoring problem behavior or not present enough to know what is happening. When leaders ignore problems, they effectively tell employees: "We don't care. This behavior is acceptable." These messages negatively affect morale for everyone else!

When leaders support employees but don't provide accountability, they often enable negative behavior by making excuses for employees. Instead of finding ways to help employees take responsibility for their own actions, enabling leaders sometimes ask others to pick up the slack from their coworkers' problematic behaviors, or they do it themselves. Because problematic behaviors are not addressed specifically, they are implicitly affirmed, and morale is negatively affected.

When accountability is high but support is low, leaders often rely on methods that are described in policies, such as written warnings, to administer discipline or punish problematic behaviors. This allows authority figures to express disapproval, but without providing the support employees may need in order to change. Punishment without support for change communicates a respect for rules, but not for people. It can send a chill through an organization, usually creating anger and defensiveness while negatively impacting morale as people take sides on whether the punishment was just.

Finally, when support and accountability are both high, leaders have the possibility of transforming behavior. This approach recognizes that change requires both the enforcement of high standards *and* the support necessary for achieving those standards. Transformative leaders work *with* employees to create change. When leaders approach accountability in this way, they demonstrate respect, compassion, and courage. While this may be difficult, it ultimately shapes individuals and teams in positive ways.

This fourth approach to accountability has clear advantages over the other three for creating a healthy workplace culture. While high levels of both accountability and support may take more time to begin with, we have learned that, in the long term, the efforts are worth it. In our own organization, when an individual has been acting in a way that doesn't fit with our values or expectations, we have a conversation with them about what is happening. We both express the need for change *and* explore what supports the employee may need to become better aligned with our values. In the rare cases when individuals have chosen not to align themselves with the organization, we've had to let them go, but we've been able to do so in ways that are understandable to them.

Dealing With Problem Behaviors

When explaining what prevents their organization from being a great place to work, many survey participants told us that their leaders don't respond well to problem behaviors. According to participants, many leaders "avoid dealing with inconsistent and detrimental employees in an effective and determined way" or "allow workers to ignore rules."

While some leaders don't do anything at all, others actively reinforce the problems. In one participant's organization, "Toxic staff are celebrated while the rest of us are seen as problems!" As a result, employees "feel uncared for" and their "motivation and self-engagement decreases." Meanwhile, "The healthy folks don't stay."

In some situations, it's even worse. One person reported, "I do not feel safe when working with some of my peers." This participant added that they had approached leadership about a problem only to find themselves "confronted in a threatening way" by the same peers they had been seeking protection from.

Fortunately, we also heard that some leaders can and do deal with problem behaviors effectively. For example, one participant wrote that their leaders "take care of problems ... respectfully and efficiently" and "address issues quickly and as they come up."

The ways in which leaders do or do not deal with problem behaviors have lasting impacts on their workplace cultures. Leaders must learn to respond quickly and thoughtfully to problem behaviors as they arise. When they do this well, they convey a spirit of care and accountability to the rest of the team and reinforce healthy workplace culture.

BEYOND CARROTS & STICKS

Unfortunately, even in healthy organizations, negative behaviors will emerge. To address these problems, some organizations still rely on a "carrot and stick" philosophy, even though this approach is antiquated and ineffective.

"Carrots," such as cash bonuses and other incentives, don't effectively encourage positive behavior change just as "sticks," or punishments, don't effectively prevent problem behaviors.

Behavioral science shows us that a paycheck, a "carrot," is only a small part of what encourages employees to perform. As Daniel H. Pink explains in his book *Drive*, the larger part of motivation is brought about by giving people autonomy, helping them achieve mastery, and connecting their behavior to a greater purpose. Pink writes: "Human beings have an innate inner drive to be autonomous, self-determined, and connected to one another. And when that drive is liberated, people achieve more and live richer lives."[7]

When we think about discipline using the same framework we use to think about rewards, we are able to see some obvious flaws in its ability to change behavior. First, a "stick" has only short-term corrective results. The threat of punishment may get someone to stop their behavior in the short term, but it doesn't get at the things that drive behavior over the long run. When the threat of a "stick" is removed, or when someone thinks they can get away with certain behaviors, they will often revert to the behavior that made sense to them in the first place.

True discipline is not about punishment, but about teaching or showing a different way of doing things. The foundational root of the word "discipline" is "to disciple" – which means that the role of discipline is to show someone a better way of acting. If we are going to disciple or discipline people, we need relationships characterized by trust and respect.

For an organization, the purpose of discipline is to get people to behave in ways that are consistent with the organization's values. When it's done well, discipline can have long-term positive effects. When it's done poorly, discipline creates additional problems, and unwanted behavior will likely reappear.

LEARNING AS A LEADER

At the heart of people-oriented leadership lies humility. We don't ever arrive! To be effective as leaders, we need to be growing and learning *continuously*. With all our responsibilities, it's easy to forget to work on *our own* development. It is common for many of us to focus on production, profit, and the worthy goal of developing employees, but these priorities should not come at the expense of our own growth.

I, Wendy, recently attended one of my son's basketball games. Though his team played hard, they weren't able to come out on top. Debriefing after the game, my son told me that he was inspired by the other team, and he wanted to become a better player. I asked him what he could do to make his goal a reality, and the answer seemed obvious to him: "I just need to get out there and play more."

All athletes know that the key to improvement is practice, but the best athletes also know *what* and *how* to practice. Before putting in too many hours of hard work, they first reflect and gather feedback from coaches or teammates to identify the specific areas that need improvement.

For my son to improve, he needed to do more than increase his time on the court. He first had to learn *how* to practice. If he simply did more of what he was already doing, without considering how to get better, his road to improvement would be much more arduous.

We advance our learning more quickly when we are intentional about what we do. We may get better over time just by "playing," but we only become truly masterful when we practice with intentionality.

Learning leadership skills is in some ways just like playing basketball. In order to grow, we must hone in on particular aspects of leadership, and we do this best when we have the time necessary to reflect on our possible areas of improvement. To grow as leaders, we need to pay attention to the particular areas of development that we have either self-identified or heard in the feedback of others.

When it comes to learning new things, it is easy to focus on the *what* and forget about the *how*. Focusing on the *how* means critically reflecting on our performance, reading widely, taking in seminars, asking others to identify our weaknesses and strengths, and engaging with leadership coaches. These are strategies that feed the mind, increase self-awareness, and generate ideas.

When we know the *how*, we are more equipped for the *what* – we are ready to go back to work and apply our newly refined skills. If the skills we have developed are effective, we will be propelled to develop them further. If they fail, we need to reconsider the *how* and try something different.

If you want to ensure that your organization is a great place to work, make leadership development a priority. Leadership development should not be a once-a-year event, but rather a continuous, ongoing process. So be sure to take the time to learn, solicit feedback, and reflect on your weaknesses and strengths.

Lessons From Our Children's Coaches

When thinking about leadership, we find it helpful to look outside our own realm of work and influence to consider the impact of leaders in other disciplines. Some of us have children involved in athletics, and we have been paying close attention to the impact and influence of their coaches.

Here are a few of the things our children said when we asked them to describe how their best coaches have inspired them to perform at a higher level:

- **"She believed in my abilities."** We all want to feel like we are good at something – that what we do brings value to the activity we are involved in. Great leaders and coaches are deliberate about demonstrating that they believe in people.

- **"He taught me things."** One of the most important responsibilities of leaders is developing the character and skills of others. Most employees want to learn and grow, and it is our job to provide such opportunities through mentorship and delegation.
- **"They were hyped up about the game."** Leaders who care passionately about their "game" inspire others to work toward a common goal. We need to be genuinely excited about what we do.
- **"They were cool."** It is more fun to be coached by someone we like, respect, and can relate to. Perhaps we aren't all considered "cool" as leaders, but we should all understand that it's important to be able to relax, relate, and have fun with our staff.
- **"She had good things to say, but she also gave me feedback that was hard to hear."** Being a nice leader is important, but so is being honest. For people to improve and excel in any domain, they need leaders who are able to give honest feedback about their performance.
- **"He paid attention to me."** We all want to matter and be noticed. Our children's coaches have manifested this in many ways, including through individual instruction and feedback. Effective leaders need to care and demonstrate that they value their employees as individuals.

What's interesting about this list that our children generated is that these are essentially the same things we adults need from our leaders. Whether you're a volunteer coach or a corporate CEO, the same basic principles apply.

MAKE YOUR LEADERSHIP INTENTIONAL

Intentional leadership means slowing down and thinking things through before speaking or acting. It is particularly important to approach potentially difficult interactions and important decisions with intentionality.

I, Randy, have tended to move too quickly from one thing to the next. I haven't always stopped long enough to gather my thoughts, and at times that has led me to say things I regret, or that I later wished I had said differently. I have also occasionally made decisions that, in hindsight, were made too hastily and without enough consideration.

A challenge for leaders of fast-paced organizations is to slow down just long enough to choose our words more carefully and make decisions that aren't rushed or arbitrary. Organizations can often attribute some of their success to their leader's ability to act and make decisions at a fast pace. However, this emphasis on doing things quickly can also make organizations vulnerable to poorly thought out decisions and ineffective interactions.

I have chosen to be more intentional, and thus I am becoming so. I have made a mindful decision to be more thoughtful in how I speak and act. Like many changes I have made to my leadership style, I have done this with deliberate effort. It is a conscious choice to do things differently.

Of course, I'm not always successful. As is the case with many changes, it is easy to fall back into old habits. When this happens, I am quick to remind myself that hasty decisions and interactions don't always end well, and I work to bring myself back to intentionality. I am getting better at it, but like most new goals, it takes time to move from intention to actual habit.

LEADERSHIP'S INFLUENCE ON CULTURE

Organizational culture is largely driven by what we as leaders value, how we behave, and in turn, what we communicate both explicitly and implicitly. Leaders help shape the ways in which employees think, behave, and feel about their work, which ultimately influences the organization's culture as a whole. Employees look to us to determine whether our values and behaviors are consistent with how we define our culture.

If you are in the process of establishing a healthy organizational culture, we encourage you to look closely at the role leadership plays. Take some time to assess your leaders and their impact. Ask staff about their experiences with direct managers. Ask managers about their interactions with the people on their teams.

A leader's influence on organizational culture cannot be overstated. Leadership and organizational culture are intricately connected, and this connection has enormous significance in helping to establish, sustain, and, if needed, change organizational culture.

QUESTIONS FOR REFLECTION

1. Think about experiences you have had with both directive and empowering managers. How have these experiences informed your own approach to leadership?

2. How do you demonstrate to employees that you care about them? In what concrete ways do you empower and offer encouragement to members of your team?

3. To what extent does your workplace pay attention to character? How might you foster character development more intentionally?

4. Where does your approach to discipline fall on the Accountability Grid? If you are not already in the "Transform" quadrant, what practical steps can you make to move in that direction?

5. How are you developing as a leader? What are some areas that you could develop further?

Build Meaningful Relationships

WORK CULTURE & HEALTHY RELATIONSHIPS

Both at home and at work, a vital part of human existence has always been and always will be the relational bonds between people. In his examination of research about loneliness, work, and the need for connection, Scott Berinato writes, "There's something almost primal about our need to be connected."[1]

In our organization, we review a variety of workplace culture themes at annual goal-setting meetings with individual employees. When we ask employees what they like most about working at ACHIEVE, their most common response is "the people." For our employees, one of the key reasons they like where they work is that they have positive relationships with each other and their leaders – they like the people they work with and for.

In our experience, one feature common to all healthy workplace cultures is a strong sense of interpersonal connection. Relationships at work ultimately provide a sense of belonging. It should be no surprise, then, that when we work to create healthy workplace cultures, we must work to create meaningful relationships.

This chapter takes a deeper look at why meaningful relationships at work go a long way toward making a workplace great. We explore how to foster a culture that encourages positive relationship development, and in particular we offer guidance for some of the trickier relationship dynamics that emerge in workplaces: the work-chitchat balance, the formation of cliques, friendships between managers and staff, and office romances.

SURVEY STATISTICS

I like the people I work with.

According to our survey, 93 percent of people who like their workplace also like the people they work with.

93%

WHY CONNECTIONS MATTER

When our children begin school, we anticipate that they will make friends, and we are sad for them if they don't. When they become teenagers, we hope they will identify with healthy peer groups, and we worry about them if they fall in with the wrong crowd. When our parents grow elderly, we worry about the impacts of isolation and loneliness. Through all of life's stages, healthy relationships are critical to personal well-being. Though we don't always make them a high priority, our relationships with coworkers are no different.

Sadly, many people's work lives are spent without a sense of meaningful connection to others. Consider that among family responsibilities, hobbies, community events, and the effort to get eight hours of sleep each night, many of us spend more waking hours in the workplace than in our own homes. This is a lot of time to spend in any single environment, especially if we aren't around coworkers we like. As one of our survey participants pointedly noted, "In most cases, you spend more time with coworkers than your own family, so why not make it a positive experience?"

People operate best in their personal and professional lives when they feel safe and secure. Consider what happens to a family when mistrust is present, when people don't get along, or when their animosity toward each other is high. The usual result is tension and an atmosphere of unhealthy energy. Family members stop sharing their thoughts and feelings, and they find excuses to avoid interactions with each other. This same dynamic occurs when tension and lack of connection exist in the workplace.

We recently did some consulting work with an organization in which the manager was often "hidden away" in his office. His small department was, in essence, left to figure things out without support. They could go days without interacting with him in any significant way.

In the absence of leadership, communication and collaboration among team members crumbled. Some team members viewed two of their coworkers as toxic, but when they brought the issue to their manager, he did not deal with it. Over time the animosity festered to the point where several employees left – first on stress leave, and then permanently. Unfortunately, this is not the only workplace we have encountered in which poor relationships have led to similar results.

Disconnection in the workplace creates barriers to communication, causing people to withdraw and withhold information because they are working in isolation. Disconnection also drives unhealthy levels of conflict because people have not established the trust necessary to work through disagreements or miscommunications. At its worst, it leads to open hostility, and people become fearful and anxious. They call in sick, take stress leave, or simply do not engage. They are certainly not able to give their best efforts, and the quality of their work is predictably compromised.

Given the human need for healthy social interaction and the consequences of unhealthy or insufficient interaction, organizations must place a high priority on fostering positive connections among staff. Yes, we can meet many of our needs for social connection outside of work, but having meaningful relationships within the workplace leads to a more fulfilling, enjoyable, and healthy work experience.

BENEFITS OF MEANINGFUL RELATIONSHIPS

Last year, I, Wendy, painted my deck. I was sure it would be a long and painful experience, and I was disheartened even before I began. On the first day, I painted for three hours before losing motivation and going for a walk. On the second day, I did the same. Before starting work on the morning of day three, I was talking on the phone with a friend and bemoaned the arduous task that lay ahead of me.

To my surprise, she showed up within the hour, paintbrush in hand. We painted, chatted, and laughed, and we worked much longer together than I would have worked on my own. By the time the sun set, my deck was beautifully restored, and my painting days were over. Just as working with a friend increased my motivation, productivity, and satisfaction, being in a workplace with a culture of strong connections can have a similar result.

In 1999, Richard Sheridan was the vice president of research and development at a software company, and he conducted a radical experiment. Rather than assigning one programmer to each computer, he required employees to work collaboratively by allowing only one computer for every two programmers.

His staff were reluctant. One programmer said the idea would lead to "blood, mayhem, [and] murder." Another announced that he was going to leave the company. But after sharing a computer for three weeks, that same employee had changed his mind. He told Sheridan, "I am having so much fun, it doesn't feel like work anymore.... I'm not sure you should pay me."[2]

Why did Sheridan's experiment work so well? Why was painting the deck with my friend so much easier than doing it alone? Because working collaboratively reduces stress while increasing motivation, productivity, satisfaction. In the following sections, we describe just a few of the benefits that come from having strong social connections at work.

Camaraderie and Increased Motivation

One of the most significant benefits of meaningful relationships at work is the feeling of camaraderie. As Edward Everett Hale is said to have stated, "Coming together is a beginning; keeping together is progress; working together is success."

Coworkers who like each other look out for each other both in good times and in times of higher stress. They experience positive energy and the power of collectively working toward a shared goal. In one study, Stanford researchers Priyanka B. Carr and Gregory M. Walton found that even when people *thought* they were working on a task with others, they persisted 48–64 percent longer than those who believed they were working alone. They reported less fatigue, performed better, had better recall of the details involved in the task, and spontaneously expressed greater enjoyment of and interest in the task. Even one to two weeks later, they freely took on similar and more challenging tasks than those who believed they had been working alone.[3]

In our consulting work, we've had the opportunity to talk with people from many different organizations, and we've noticed that workers frequently cite camaraderie as a reason for coming to work. Sometimes it is the only reason they still work where they do. In our experience, it's clear that people work harder and longer when they are part of a group effort.

Increased Productivity

Both at ACHIEVE and in our consulting work with other organizations, we have seen that when people work with others, they are more productive. Most of us value our coworkers' opinions of us, and we want to be seen as significant contributors. We are more willing to spend time and effort on tasks when we enjoy the company of those working alongside us and when we value their appraisal of our work.

Describing her workplace, one of our survey participants wrote, "Our motto is, 'we work hard and play hard.'" Coworkers who like each other also usually encourage, praise, and validate each other. We know that praise and validation feel good, and when employees feel good, they are typically more productive.

As Berinato writes, "It stands to reason that if lonely workers are less healthy, they'll be less productive and less engaged."[4] His statement should be taken as a warning: it is imperative to ensure that our employees are not lonely at work, but rather connected to their coworkers.

Reduced Stress

Most of us have had the unpleasant experience of coming home to a loved one who is grumpy and irritable after a stressful day at work – many of us have probably even been that person ourselves. When we are happy at work, we tend to be happier at home. Home life certainly affects work life, but the opposite is true as well.

While it is impossible to completely eliminate the possibility of stressful days at work, having colleagues to lean on for added support can often make tough days more manageable. Whether it's words of advice or a smile from a coworker, small moments of companionship and personal connection increase happiness while reducing stress. When we have healthy relationships, our colleagues at work will notice when we are struggling and, as friends often do, offer support that reduces our stress. One survey participant summarized this idea well when they wrote: "We work as a team where everyone is equally important. When 'life' happens and one of us isn't 100 percent, we always pick up the slack for each other and make sure we meet our goals."

SURVEY RESPONSES

The People

When we asked what factors make their organization a great place to work, many of our survey participants zeroed in on *relationships*. Some simply said "the people" or "my colleagues." Other participants went into specifics. For example, some mentioned the work ethic of their coworkers:

"I work with lots of great, committed folks."

"Everyone is engaged."

"It's great to rub shoulders with high-achieving, dedicated, hard-working, innovative coworkers."

Others highlighted the value of feeling supported:

"People appreciate me."

"Everyone cheers each other on."

"I feel well respected and enjoy interacting with staff who are generally warm, friendly, and caring."

At the same time, participants also usually brought up "people" when describing the factors preventing their workplace from being great:

"There are a couple bad apples that make the environment toxic."

"Two individuals have created an office with low morale."

"A few 'dead bodies' bring morale and expectations down."

You'll notice that just a few people can have a significant negative impact on workplace morale. But what is it in particular that these people do to hold back the entire workplace? When participants went into specifics (which they often did), they consistently named three things: "negativity," "cliques," and "gossip." Here's what people had to say about why these behaviors continue:

"Although there are policies in place, there are no consequences to actions."

"Poor behaviors are being reinforced by not being challenged or resolved."

"Not all managers are confident in dealing with the uncomfortable aspects of employment as swiftly as they could and should."

Statements like these tell us that employees want leaders to more actively respond to the negative behaviors that impact relationships. Some participants also told us they want more opportunities to form better relationships:

> "It would be nice to go to work in the morning and see everyone, or even eat lunch together, but we are not set up this way."
> "I believe that if we all worked closer together it would benefit us."
> "Taking time to get to know each other's interests and passions would allow for healthy relationships to form."

People are the best part of work for some people, and they are the worst part of work for others. To create a workplace where people like to work, organizations should focus on hiring employees who are enjoyable to be with, skilled and passionate about their work, and supportive of their team members. Leaders should provide opportunities for workers to interact so they can build stronger relationships and support each other. Leaders should also respond quickly to problem behaviors as they arise.

HOW TO CREATE MEANINGFUL RELATIONSHIPS

Once we recognize the value of meaningful relationships at work, the question that follows is, "How do we create and maintain workplaces that foster camaraderie?"

Quite simply, social connections at work are fostered in the same way that they are anywhere else – by people spending time together. To build strong relationships, we need time to talk, joke around, eat, play, and work hard together.

Meaningful relationships require both enjoyable and sometimes even difficult shared experiences. Think about what happens when a healthy workplace faces an emergency. All of a sudden, everyone begins to work collaboratively to respond to the situation, regardless of their areas of responsibility. The walls of separation created by titles and departments are quickly broken down. When coworkers experience an event together, they feel more connected as a result.

Above all else, remember that while relationships are a natural part of human experience, they don't often happen without effort. As with many things in life, if we devote time and energy toward forging relationships in our places of work, our efforts will eventually be rewarded.

In the following few sections, we identify some specific things organizations can do to foster positive relationships.

Provide a Variety of Ways to Connect

Our workplaces become truly welcoming when they reflect the diversity of ways that different people connect. An extroverted manager who designs the office space, runs meetings, and plans social events to suit their own preferences is sure to exclude those on the team who are more introverted. As we make space for relationships to develop, we must remember that different people have different preferences for how and when they connect. For instance, some people enjoy time for quiet conversation, while others prefer the exuberance of a party, and still others would rather connect over an activity.

Spend Time Together

Don't just work together – eat, drink, play, or volunteer together as well. Social gatherings such as holiday parties and summer barbeques are opportunities for leaders and employees alike to engage with each other as peers. They are opportunities to interact in purely social ways and learn about the lives of colleagues outside the workplace.

At ACHIEVE, in addition to social gatherings, we spend time together by participating in community events. We attend fundraisers for local not-for-profits, and we participate in rallies and events for causes that align with our values.

Many organizations rely on holiday parties to foster social connection.

These events are often loud and filled with activity, and they usually involve alcohol. While many employees may enjoy this type of get-together, some do not. As you plan events that will facilitate bonding in your organization, ensure that there is some variety over the course of the year.

When considering the location of a weekly drinks-after-work gathering, remember that some people can't or won't go to bars due to preference, religion, or addiction. Transportation to events might pose a problem for people without cars. The time of gatherings might affect people with kids. The location may not be accessible to people with mobility issues. These dynamics should always be considered as you work to provide opportunities for *all* employees to interact with the larger group in settings suitable to their preferences.

Increase Face Time

If your organization's employees don't all work together in the same space every day, consider posting pictures of staff members in newsletters, on your website, and around your office.

At ACHIEVE, many of our trainers and some of our staff live in other parts of the country. In order to facilitate connection, we put together a regular newsletter that includes a section featuring pictures and personal stories from people within our organization. We know that, due to a phenomenon called the "mere exposure effect," when people regularly see someone – even if it's only a photo – they tend to like them more.

Move Away From Your Desk and Devices

Just as we don't meet our neighbors if we stay in our houses, we don't interact with our coworkers or employees if we're always working at our desks.

Those of us who are in leadership roles certainly do not inspire employees to interact with their coworkers when we create bubbles around ourselves or bury ourselves in work. We should instead lead by example and model open, friendly, and inclusive behaviors.

All of us – employees and leaders alike – should walk into the workplace with our eyes up and phones away. We should eat in the lunch room phoneless when others are there, leave our phones in our pockets during those few minutes before staff meetings, and avoid the temptation to check them the minute the meeting is done. Although they may feel awkward for some, these moments when we are tempted to escape into the virtual world are opportunities to connect with those around us.

Be Mindful of Space

Organizations should provide welcoming spaces where people can gather with ease and comfort. Staff rooms should be places where people can meet, unwind, and spend a bit of time enjoying each other's company without the demands of work.

Keeping workspaces tidy and providing comfortable seating, access to snacks, cozy retreat areas, plants, artwork, and warm décor can go a long way in bringing people together. A bench just outside the front door can be a place to get some fresh air, take a break, and have a conversation with a coworker. Thoughtful consideration for how workstations are oriented relative to other areas can enhance interaction and productivity. A kitchen, while serving a basic function, can also be a vital social hub.

In our own organization, we're intentional about providing a multitude of ways for people to naturally connect with each other. We want our office to be a space where people can easily bump into each other throughout the day rather than only seeing people from other departments at monthly company-wide meetings. To facilitate these types of mini-connections, we have gathering areas where we can all meet informally or formally. We also purposefully have only one water cooler and coffee maker so that people naturally congregate in the same area.

Though these meeting areas are important, we also realize that our employees need spaces with minimal distractions to allow for intense focus. As such, we ensure there are places for people to retreat for quiet, uninterrupted work.

As you consider your own office and building design, ask yourself whether your workspace is conducive to healthy relationships.

Feeling the Squeeze

In our consulting work, we have often seen the negative ways in which space can impact relationships. In one memorable situation, six case managers, who dealt with complex and stressful issues over the phone, were crammed into an office designed for about three people. During the work day, they regularly spoke with clients about personal and confidential matters, which required focus and an environment free of distraction.

Due to the intense nature of their work, some of them needed to be able to debrief their stressful experiences with their colleagues and have a little fun. However, due to their close quarters, their competing needs for focused time with clients and opportunities to debrief led to very unhealthy conflict. Both needs were real, but the space didn't allow them to have both needs met. In this case, we helped the management team see that the conflict among the staff could not be fully addressed until the office space issue was dealt with.

Learn Together

One way to give an opportunity for staff to connect with each other is to schedule a development day pertaining to a topic that relates to everyone in the organization. The most effective learning opportunities for relationship development are those that are not solely focused on job skills but also include personal development. For example, training in areas such as emotional intelligence or stress management can apply to everyone in the workplace.

Sometimes a change of pace lets team members break out of their roles, allowing them to meet others and connect over new content and ideas. At the same time, those in attendance learn valuable skills to apply to their work.

You may want to consider hiring a professional facilitator for your professional development day. As facilitators ourselves, we have noticed that it is an advantage to lead groups without having any preconceived notions about the connections, or lack thereof, among them. Coming from outside the organization allows us to get people working together in ways they are not accustomed to and to ask questions that may be difficult for an insider to ask.

Understand Each Other's Work

Look for opportunities for people from various departments to work together intermittently. This fosters connections by allowing them to better understand and appreciate each other's work. Though every employee likely can't be familiar with every task in a workplace, it is helpful for everyone to have a general understanding of what their colleagues are responsible for.

At ACHIEVE, when new employees are oriented, they spend time in each department learning about the various roles of their new colleagues. At our monthly meetings, each department reports on things that are interesting, challenging, or important for others to know. In this way, we work to remind all employees that they are part of a larger team.

SURVEY STATISTICS

I have fun at work.

According to our survey, 83 percent of people who like their workplace also have fun at work.

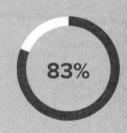

83%

Give Fun Its Rightful Place

There is much truth in the saying, "Laughter is the best medicine." Laughter releases endorphins, increases oxygen intake, elevates the pain threshold, eases stress, and brings people together. It's important to remember to have fun. Life is too short to be serious all the time.

In our organization, one way we have fun is by celebrating odd and interesting events on the calendar, such as National Cream-Filled Doughnut Day and National High Five Day. We often pause for a moment to laugh and ponder the origin of these days while enjoying a cream-filled doughnut or giving each other high fives. These short little diversions throughout the week increase not only laughter but social connection as well.

SURVEY RESPONSES

Taking Time for Fun

As a busy leader, you might wonder whether having fun with employees really is a priority. You may feel that you don't have time to joke around at staff meetings, much less hang out with coworkers on coffee breaks. You may even be concerned that too much fun is distracting and reduces productivity.

In the written responses to the survey questions, "What about your workplace contributes to making it a great place to work?" and "What about your workplace hinders it from being as great a place to work as it could be?" *fun at work* was a common theme. Interestingly, survey participants frequently emphasized that they both have fun *and* get work done:

"Regular staff meetings are fun and efficient."
"While I work in a fast-paced workplace, my coworkers make the job really fun."
"I can consistently rely on the people I work with to accomplish

their responsibilities efficiently and effectively while still finding opportunities to have fun."

One takeaway here is that some people like having fun when it's balanced with hard work. Fun and work go hand in hand because having fun both boosts productivity and brings people together. One participant felt that having fun was exactly what their leaders needed to do in order to build the trust his workplace desperately needed:

> "Our organization's management coincidentally changed at the same time we went through serious layoffs about five years ago. This management team has remained silent with many of their actions. They're just quiet people, but this is interpreted as being sneaky and distrustful of staff. If only management would just be regular people and *have fun* with staff to show they're really human after all."

As a leader, if you feel like you don't have as much time for fun as you would like, there's good news. One participant wrote that even when leaders *attempt* to have fun, that effort can go a long way. In their words, "The boss joins in the fun when he can."

Our survey participants seem to want us all to encourage playfulness in our workplaces while finding a balance between having fun and expecting productivity. Leaders should join in the fun when we can while encouraging others to do the same.

MAINTAINING APPROPRIATE BOUNDARIES

While having meaningful relationships at work is important, research also indicates that, in some instances, these relationships can hinder productivity and happiness.[5] When our coworkers are stressed, distracted, or disinterested in their work, they may have negative impacts on us and our own work.

It is important that organizations encourage social connections, but they must also be clear about expected boundaries. The rest of this chapter highlights a few areas where boundaries might need to be established to help maintain a healthy workplace culture.

Cliques at Work

Although we want to encourage relationships, we also want to actively discourage the formation of cliques in our workplaces. When cliques do form, leaders need to deal with them promptly and effectively.

Cliques are exclusive groups of people who share common interests. They are surrounded by thick relational walls that are difficult to penetrate. Cliques usually develop identities based on shared interests or functions, such as The Friday Beer Group, The Potluck Club, The Management Team, The Smokers' Group, or The Sales Team.

Most people enjoy being part of a group, but when groups turn into cliques, there can be some serious downsides. When coworkers socialize in and outside of work, those who are not part of the group often feel excluded. Usually the exclusion is not deliberate, but sometimes it is. Regardless of their intent, cliques are just as damaging and demoralizing in the workplace as they are in schools and other social settings.

In addition to social exclusion, cliques within organizations also unfortunately encourage like-mindedness and groupthink. Irving Janis, who coined the term groupthink, says that it tends to weaken mental efficiency while reducing the group members' capacity to make both rational decisions and objective moral judgments of each other.[6]

When people within cliques make decisions, they are highly motivated to fit in and maintain their status in the group. This means that they do not challenge potentially unhealthy decisions for fear of upsetting others. This can be especially problematic when the leaders of an organization form a clique, as their decisions have a greater impact on the organization as a whole.

Rather than gaining the benefit of each person's insights, cliques are typically dominated by those with the strongest voices. People in cliques often bow to the influence of the leaders of the group, deferring to their opinions and ideas. When workplaces are dominated by cliques, they lose the benefit of having many voices contribute to conversations and decisions.

As we have often seen in our conflict management work, cliques also tend to perpetuate conflict. This is due to the fact that clique members protect each other. When one group member is threatened, the others come to their aid. Given the dynamics of groupthink, if one person in a clique dislikes someone outside the group, their fellow clique members will often take sides, and soon the whole group is united against another person.

This can be incredibly destructive for the wider workplace and team environment. When conflicts arise, cliques act as blocs of power. They fight for their side rather than for the good of the whole group.

In healthy workplace cultures, people still form groups, but they pay conscious attention to keeping boundaries porous. Here are some strategies for preventing the formation of cliques in your workplace:

- **Promote awareness.** When communicating with your team, highlight the value of cross-connection throughout the workplace. Be clear that your organization promotes friendships *and* inclusivity.
- **Create opportunities to work together.** Pay attention to groupings in your workplace. A leader's role includes ensuring that staff have working relationships across different teams and departments. At ACHIEVE, we regularly ask staff to work on projects connected to the work of different departments or teams.
- **Provide coaching.** When you see the potential for groups to become cliques, meet with individuals and discuss this openly. Highlight the difference between social groups and cliques. Remind staff of the organization's expectations for inclusivity and cross-connection.

Balancing Work and Chitchat

Both I, Michael, and my wife regularly work from home. As our teens have started attending university, there have been more and more people working in our home, and we've discovered that everyone has different social needs in order to get work done. When writing or studying, my oldest son rarely comes out of his room. My youngest daughter, on the other hand, will do anything to avoid studying alone. She pauses frequently to talk to whoever is around, which irritates my wife because *she* wants to be surrounded by other people but also wants them to be quiet. I mostly like to be alone, but later in the day, the solitude drives me to distraction, and I seek out others for interaction.

While most of us don't have to manage family dynamics at work, we still have to pay attention to the varying needs of staff. Part of this means ensuring that there is a balance of work and chitchat.

In our organization, we view camaraderie among staff as positive, and we work to maintain an environment where it is possible. This sort of warm and friendly work environment inevitably leads to a certain amount of non-work-related conversation. From our perspective, this is actually a good thing. We believe it's important to check in with people about their upcoming weekend or vacation plans. We encourage this, and we think of these times as an investment in our organization's culture that will increase personal and organizational productivity in the long term.

However, conversations must be kept in balance. When quick chats regularly turn into full-blown conversations during work time, leaders may need to step in and enable individuals to set boundaries around the amount of conversation that is good for both them and the organization.

We believe that personal connection and work are both important and exist in dynamic tension with each other. They are interrelated, and when they are balanced, they result in productivity and fulfilling relationships. Fundamentally, we need employees to do their work in order to accomplish the vision of the organization. If there is too much chitchat, work begins to suffer. On the other hand, if there is too much work and not enough social interaction, the fuel for work that comes from social connection decreases.

Leaders need to monitor both connection and work, and they must periodically recalibrate the balance between the two. Here are a few suggestions to set the stage for a healthy balance between work and meaningful relationships:

- **Talk openly about boundaries.** Every workplace should have its own understanding about how much workplace chitchat is acceptable. For example, in our workplace a two- to five-minute impromptu chat unrelated to work is acceptable, but a ten- to fifteen-minute conversation usually is not.
- **Take breaks.** Most workplaces allocate a certain amount of time for employees to rest, recuperate, and socialize. It's important to encourage employees to use this time to catch up with each other and follow up on the brief conversations that were started during the day.
- **Give individual feedback.** If a particular employee is oversharing or routinely engaging in long conversations, leadership may need to intervene and coach that person individually.
- **Give group feedback.** When chitchat increases beyond its ideal level within a group, gently state your observations and remind employees about the importance of balance. When giving this feedback, be sure to affirm healthy social interaction and openly discuss parameters. Otherwise, you may inadvertently dampen social connections, which, in turn, will diminish productivity and engagement.

As always, the key is *balance*. Work and healthy social engagements are not opposites, but rather complementary aspects of organizations that are full of happy and engaged people. When this balance is achieved, it drives organizational health and productivity.

Friendships Between Managers and Staff

For many of us, coworkers can become lifelong friends. But friendships between managers and those they supervise can often be more complicated. Should we encourage these kinds of relationships? A close relationship between a manager and someone they supervise can certainly be complicated and confusing in that it may hinder the manager's ability to address performance issues. However, these relationships can also be rewarding if they are approached in the right way.

We encourage organizations to have conversations with their management teams about how to navigate friendships with those they supervise. Open conversation reduces ambiguity and allows you to decide what is best for your organizational culture. Your conversation should cover the following:

- What are the risks and benefits of having friendships with those you supervise? Make sure to think through both sides of this question.
- How will you deal with perceptions of favoritism if someone in management is supervising a friend? What can you do to prevent both favoritism and the perception of favoritism?
- What are ways you can keep relationships with coworkers separate from personal friendships?
- When someone is promoted and becomes the manager of their former colleagues, how will you help them navigate the changes this creates in their relationships?

Each organizational culture will have its own unique answers to these questions. The most important goal of this conversation is to develop clarity. Once the management team has developed clarity, write down the principles you have determined that managers and employees should follow, and share them with the rest of the organization.

On a Personal Note...

I, Randy, am Wendy's manager. She and I are also great friends. Our families regularly get together for social gatherings, and our children are close as well. We were friends prior to our work with ACHIEVE. Throughout our relationship, I've learned a few things about being friends with someone you are supervising.

For me, it has worked best to keep a clear distinction between our relationship as friends and our relationship as coworkers. When we are at work, my friend is my employee first and foremost. This means that I manage and give feedback in the same way that I would for anyone else. Outside of the work environment, we are equalized as friends. As in any healthy relationship, we have a good level of respect for each other both at work and after hours.

Romance at the Office

If you have worked in an organization with more than a few people for long enough, you may have witnessed an office romance – or maybe you've been part of one yourself. Statistics vary, but a quick web search pulls up multiple sources suggesting that approximately 40 percent of workers have dated a coworker at some point in their career – and a good number of those relationships have resulted in marriage.[7] That's a lot of people romancing at the office! So, is this a good thing or a bad thing?

Romance feels great to the people who are falling in love. It tends to make them happier, healthier, and more motivated to be at work. However, it often creates distraction from work tasks – especially in the beginning stages of the relationship or if it turns sour.

Things get much trickier when the relationship involves a supervisor and their subordinate. Coworkers sometimes perceive a conflict of interest in that the subordinate may gain an unfair level of influence. After all, how can a manager provide anything like an objective performance evaluation for an employee they are romantically involved with?

When workplace romances turn sour, the fallout often affects others in the workplace. Colleagues may be asked to take sides, creating cliques around the estranged partners. At best, people must put energy toward avoiding offense or awkward situations. This often results in extra time and effort to keep the two people apart, such as not having meetings where the two will be present or assigning tasks so as to not have the former couple placed on the same team.

In reality, asking whether office romance is a good thing or a bad thing isn't the right question. Given the shockingly high prevalence of workplace romance, we are better off asking ourselves, "Are we prepared for office romance when it happens?"

The impact of workplace romance varies greatly depending on who is involved, whether they work together directly, and how big the organization is as a whole. In small organizations, it may not be possible to put distance between a romancing pair, while large organizations may be able to move people or change lines of accountability. Given the differences among workplaces, a one-size-fits-all approach doesn't make sense.

At ACHIEVE, we believe that prohibition generally backfires by driving relationships underground and making them harder to understand, respond to, and manage appropriately. Instead of prohibiting romantic relationships, we have a policy for responding to office romance, which includes what we will do if a relationship develops between a supervisor and their subordinate.

Here are some tips for how to prepare for the inevitability of an office romance:

- **Plan your response.** Have a discussion as a management team about how to best manage office romance. Be sure to record the results of this discussion in a written document. We recommend consulting with staff for their input and feedback as you draft a policy. Ensure that this information is included in your employee orientation process.

- **Be clear about supervisor–supervisee romance.** Make sure your policy addresses how the organization will respond if a supervisor forms a relationship with an employee who they supervise. In most cases, it may be best to discourage these types of relationships, as they are fraught with the potential for negative impacts on the workplace whether they go well for the couple or not.

- **Speak with those in the relationship.** When a relationship does happen, have both parties sign a consensual relationship agreement. Encourage those involved to keep personal issues outside of work, just as all staff are expected to. Let them know that personal relationships should not impact work performance and that poor performance will always be taken seriously.

When it comes to workplace romance, the best approach is to prepare for the inevitable, encourage transparency, and discourage romantic relationships between supervisors and those they supervise.

INVEST IN RELATIONSHIPS

Relationships and social connections matter in both our personal and professional lives. Wherever we find them, positive relationships make us happy. The opposite is also true. When relationships are absent or unhealthy, we do not have the interest or energy required to go above and beyond. We move toward individualism, and our priority becomes simply getting to the end of the day. Yes, we may focus on the work itself, but not in the same wholehearted way that we could in the context of healthy, energizing relationships.

One of our survey participants accurately pointed out, "Working toward more meaningful connections with each other takes time, but when people relate to each other on a deeper level, things fall into place." When we like the people we work with, when we experience camaraderie and collaboration, our personal satisfaction increases and our experience of work becomes enjoyable. Organizations will flourish when they invest in creating a culture that fosters meaningful relationships.

QUESTIONS FOR REFLECTION

1. What evidence do you see of meaningful relationships at your workplace? In what ways do people connect throughout the day? Is everyone included?
2. What opportunities exist for people to work together on projects in your workplace? What are some ways you can increase collaboration throughout your organization?
3. Do you have a warm and welcoming work environment? If not, how can you change your physical workspace to create a better atmosphere? Are there sufficient common areas for people to meet with each other?
4. When and how often do people laugh in your workplace? How might you encourage more fun?
5. How well do people understand the social boundaries around cliques, chitchat, and romance in your workplace? Are all employees sufficiently aware of your organization's protocols concerning these boundaries?

Create Peak Performing Teams

WORKING TOGETHER

Most of the meaningful and important things an organization accomplishes are not done individually, but within the context of teams. Working together with other talented individuals motivates and inspires us to not only improve our own performance, but to increase our team's performance as well. This is because we all desire to be part of something bigger than ourselves and do good work that is appreciated by others. Peak performing teams are important to healthy cultures because they are more likely to make people take pride in their organization and its accomplishments.

Peak performing teams are groups that are very productive and consistently produce high-quality products or services. They are made up of members who identify with the group and are highly motivated, diverse, and empowered. Members of peak performing teams know who they can rely on for which tasks. They know that there is room for disagreement, that their strong relationships will carry them through stormy times, and that each person will contribute their best efforts.

Teamwork reinforces the culture of an organization, whether it is healthy or not. As people work together, they share cultural knowledge with each other. Longer-term employees can share their acquired wisdom with newer employees, who can then test their ideas and learn which behaviors are acceptable.

Unfortunately, some organizations fail to realize the full power of collaboration. Instead of having cohesive groups of people working together, they have collections of individuals working on their own. When people work solely with individual goals in mind, the full potential of their team or organization will never be realized.

At ACHIEVE, we get tremendous amounts of work done in short periods of time, but this does not just happen organically. It is deliberate and methodical – it's a result of collaboration between individuals on teams and collaboration between those teams. Year after year, we produce innovative and high-quality products and services because of peak performing teams.

New staff who come into our organization are often surprised by the pace at which we make decisions and implement ideas. This pace inspires them, and they are excited to work in such an environment. We are focused on creating and sustaining peak performing teams in our organization not only because they produce more and higher quality work, but because we have seen that the best employees want to work with others in organizations that get things done. Peak performing teams are part of what makes our organization a great place to work.

This chapter is about understanding why and how peak performing teams contribute to a healthy workplace culture and learning how to harness the power of teams in your organization. We'll explore how teams are best developed, what pitfalls to avoid along the way, and how to benefit from the wisdom of groups. We refer to teams in a broad sense – teams may include small departments or groups of people, but in smaller organizations, the workplace as a whole might be considered a team.

THE POWER OF COLLECTIVE INTELLIGENCE

We are often told to avoid following the crowd. In words often attributed to George Bernard Shaw, "The minority is sometimes right; the majority is always wrong." But sometimes a crowd can provide insights that an individual cannot. Francis Galton, a brilliant researcher in the early 1900s, demonstrated this point perfectly. He came across a contest at a country fair in which fairgoers were invited to guess the weight of an ox after it was butchered. The person whose guess was the most accurate would be the winner. Over eight hundred people participated.

Galton found that, though individual responses varied substantially, the average of the responses was remarkably close to the actual weight of the ox.[1] In this instance, the group was correct! This ability to reach a better decision as a group than as individuals is known as "group wisdom" or "collective intelligence."

Many of us like to think we avoid following the crowd in our lives, but the truth is that most of us look to group wisdom to guide many of our actions. We read book reviews on Amazon or Goodreads to decide what to read next, and most of us have consulted TripAdvisor or read restaurant reviews to help us decide where to stay or eat on our holidays. We assume that there will be some naysayers among the reviewers, and that a few evaluations will be excessively glowing, but we have confidence that the voice of the majority is representative of reality. This is collective intelligence at work in our everyday lives.

In order for organizations to harness the power of collective intelligence, team members first need time to become comfortable with each other. As one of our survey participants reported, longevity tends to increase team performance: "We have long-term employees and deal with very little turnover. This can inherently make it easier to communicate effectively with others, as we have come to understand how to adapt our style to meet the other's needs."

In an article titled "Why Teams Don't Work," Diane Coutu explains, "The problem almost always is not that a team gets stale but, rather, that it doesn't have the chance to settle in."[2] She goes on to describe research that confirms that prolonged group experience is directly tied to productivity. One study she cites reveals that 73 percent of airline errors or incidents occur when crews are flying together for the first time. Teams need experience working together to be successful, and this cannot be gained without sufficient time.

Just as a crowd can more accurately guess the weight of an ox, so too can a team's collective intelligence produce better results over time than an individual's efforts. However, in order to develop peak performing teams and reap the benefits of collective intelligence, we as leaders need to give conscious thought to how we develop our teams.

SURVEY RESPONSES

The Impact of Healthy Teams

When we asked people to identify the factors that make their workplaces great, or prevent them from being great, the significance of healthy teams became very apparent. For many survey participants, there was a clear connection between their sense of well-being at work and the health of their teams. Participants made statements like these about why their teams make their workplaces great:

> "I appreciate being on a team where every person has high integrity, dedication, and passion for the work."
> "We work so well as a team. We all take our responsibilities seriously."
> "Being able to encourage, support, work alongside, and problem solve with each other as a team is amazing."

Team diversity also came up often. Many participants pointed out that their teams leverage the various talents of team members.

> "People are valued for their diverse talents."
> "We're a multi-generational team with a mix of genders and perspectives that complement one another well. Everyone's tasks are clearly organized and separated from the others', but we are all able to support one another in projects as well."

"Everyone brings something different, which is super important because it allows diversity and strength in the service we provide."

We also heard from others who identified the lack of teamwork as a significant factor preventing their workplaces from being great:

"We don't communicate with each other. We don't know what each other's projects are and don't work as a team."
"There are individuals with their own agendas who are not willing to cooperate or come together as a team."

When organizations do not make it a priority to develop healthy teams, they cannot hope to have a workplace culture that people like. However, as our survey participants pointed out, there are some simple things you can do to help your teams work together well: define roles, value people for their diversity, encourage them to contribute their strengths, and practice cooperation and communication.

HOW TO CREATE TEAMS

Team-building retreats and workshops have become the norm for organizations seeking to foster team spirit. Team-building days typically include some combination of the following: a game to break people out of their everyday roles, an exercise that helps build trust among team members, a challenge that requires everyone's participation to be successful, and a fun activity to build group identity.

In our work at ACHIEVE, clients often ask us to facilitate these sorts of team-building activities. There is nothing wrong with these activities, particularly when the emphasis is on having fun and being together. However, as we always tell our clients, activities like these are best when they are used in conjunction with practical conversations about how teams relate and work together.

Teams are healthiest when they are made up of people who feel a strong connection to each other *and* to the organization. As we explain in the following sections, leaders must harness the power of team motivation, foster identification and interdependence, embrace diversity, and empower teams to make decisions.

HARNESS THE POWER OF TEAM MOTIVATION

When organizations have high levels of motivation among individuals and teams, an infectious, energizing spirit overtakes everyone. People work well together and achieve higher levels of productivity as a result. As one of our survey participants reported: "On our team, no one is perfect, but we interact very effectively. We mesh together well. The result is balance, efficiency, and productivity."

One of the most overlooked yet powerful motivators in the workplace is the social motivation that teams provide. When we are determining how to behave in social situations, we look for cues from the people around us. People demonstrate through their actions what is acceptable in an organization and what is not. Tapping into the positive elements of social motivation is an important aspect of creating peak performing teams.

One of the more fascinating studies about social motivation we reviewed considered what would motivate hotel guests to reuse their towels.[3] In the first trial, the research team began by placing cards in hotel rooms, reminding guests of the environmental benefits of reusing towels. However, they discovered that this was relatively ineffective.

In the second trial, when the research team informed people that *most* hotel guests (75 percent) reused their towels, they saw a significant increase in the number of guests who reused their towels. It seems that many of us are motivated less by a concern for the environment and more by a need to fit in with those around us. The message in the second trial gave a clear indication of what was socially acceptable and what was not, and it resulted in a significant change.

Social motivators are present in our workplaces as well. When employees see others working on tasks and projects that are exciting and require high levels of commitment, they typically want to be involved in those activities as well. When working effectively as a team, staff feed off of each other in positive ways to sustain their motivation. When effective teamwork is absent, however, some people may seek out social motivation in a different workplace altogether. As one survey participant wrote, "Teamwork is essential, and without it many of our staff would not continue to work here."

Highly motivated individuals want to be surrounded by others who are highly motivated. They crave the energy of collaboration, and once they are used to it, they won't settle for less. At ACHIEVE, we have seen how new hires are, in a way, pressured into joining a culture of peak performance. It's as though existing employees are telling them: "We are motivated and productive workers. We want you to get on board with the way things are done here."

An additional benefit of peak performing teams is that highly motivated coworkers tend to manage each other. When the majority of people in an organization are motivated, others will either raise their level to match it – on their own or through positive peer pressure – or they will leave. When most people are productive and working hard to fulfill the mission and vision of the organization, they set a standard that comes to be expected of others.

FOSTER IDENTIFICATION

When people feel that they are a part of a team, it becomes an important part of their identity. While identifying too strongly with a group can lead to negative consequences such as groupthink, associating and collaborating with others is an essential part of our human identities. The principle of "identification" suggests that we bond more closely with people who we perceive to be most like us. When others have personality traits or interests that are similar to our own, we often feel a sense of connection with them. The greater the number of identifying characteristics a group can find, the more powerful the sense of identification for its members will be.

Our sense of connection with others often comes through identifying as part of a group. We create our personal identities through our associations with our families, our religious groups, the sports teams we support, and our workplaces. These groups provide reference points for our values, help direct our behaviors, and shape who we understand ourselves to be. Professional sports teams capitalize on this principle to great effect. In most major cities, you don't have to look hard to find bumper stickers, hats, or jerseys that support the local team. People make small talk about their team and feel connected by displaying its symbols.

In a similar way, the more an employee identifies with their workplace, the more committed and connected they will feel. In the following sections, we explore some ideas for capitalizing on the power of identification in the workplace.

Let People Know Their Team Is Special

Everyone wants to feel like they are part of a worthwhile group. As a leader, it is your job to ensure that employees know their teams are important. Highlighting the importance of teams begins during the hiring process. Even while interviewing candidates, you can emphasize the value that your organization places on team membership by including the candidate's potential coworkers in the interview process.

Even before new hires begin, you can show them that it is a privilege to work for their new organization as a member of a particular team. I, Eric, have always enjoyed calling a successful applicant and congratulating them on their new job. In a recent call, a successful candidate expressed her excitement about coming to work with us. She mentioned how good it felt to leave an industry that had drained her and instead to enter a caring work environment. As I responded to her excitement during the call, I mentioned that I consider it a privilege to work for ACHIEVE, and I hoped she would as well. It was important to me that she knew she was joining a special group of people.

After the hiring process, you can continue to highlight that the team is special in simple ways. Routinely talk with employees about how they are cooperating with each other, and identify the positive results that their collaboration has brought to the team.

When customers are pleased, your staff should know this. When sales are up, staff should be aware. When new products or services are rolled out, employees should be informed. By telling stories about how your team has succeeded, you build a sense of collective identity that emphasizes why it is a privilege to be a part of your team.

Emphasize a Shared History and Future

It's hard to identify with a group when we don't know its history. As leaders, it's important to regularly talk about the history of our organization: where it came from, how it has grown, how it has changed, and how it continues to evolve. Who are its founders? Why did they start the organization? What makes the organization unique?

At ACHIEVE, we have noticed that employees are captivated when we share stories from the early years of our organization. Having a better understanding of when and why we did what we did helps to build collective identity.

Imagining the shared future that is right in front of us is just as important. Leaders should regularly share what they are doing that is new and exciting. Explain what projects are on the horizon, where the organization is struggling, and how it is hoping to develop and grow. These kinds of conversations bind people together.

The Value of Origin Stories

When I, Michael, worked at a manufacturing company, the human resources department drew heavily on the company's origin story. They made it into a documentary, which became part of the orientation for new employees. The documentary told the story of the company's founder, an immigrant who had been dissatisfied with the way he was treated working for a local retailer. As a result, he left his job to make wooden ladders in his basement. The documentary showed worn, black and white photographs of the founder in his first factory – a converted barn – during the 1940s. In a voiceover, the aging man himself told viewers about the birth of the company. By the end of the documentary, we had seen him progress from a beleaguered bottom-rung clerk to the founder of an organization with a mission. It was inspiring because now, as new employees, we were part of the story too.

Most organizations have interesting origin stories if you are willing to ask. However, few seem to have taken the time to share their stories publicly. Origin stories humanize the founders of the organization and allow employees and clients alike to relate to its purpose. In essence, they enrich the purpose statements that organizations have worked so hard to craft. For this reason, we believe that as you work to articulate your purpose, you should find ways to tell your origin story as well.

Once you have written your story, find ways to share it. Tell it in a newsletter or on your website; include it in new staff orientation sessions and client events. You should see your story as a powerful opportunity to engage others. You can find ACHIEVE's origin story on our website at www.achievecentre.com, under the heading, "Our Story."

Focus on Values That Are Core to Your Team's Identity

When people identify with named team values, they are more likely to identify with the team. In our organization, we have named productivity as a core value. On the surface, this may seem like an obvious attribute that all organizations should strive for – and even something that should be expected but need not be said. However, we have intentionally chosen to name productivity as one of the core values that makes us unique. In this way, we clearly state the expectation that all employees will be productive while at the same time affirming that they are part of an exceptional group that is especially productive.

Because we clearly identify productivity as one of our organization's core values, our employees are able to align their personal values with those of the organization. This creates a connection point: The organization is productive, and I am productive. I am compatible and identify with a team of others who share my values.

Identifiable and shared values create reference points for teams. If team values are not named, people will identify with the values that seem apparent to them, whether those are positive values or not. When leaders are purposeful about emphasizing specific values, they create the conditions for employees to identify with the team in healthy ways. As a leader, you should emphasize the values that are most important for your particular team. Point them out when you see them in action and affirm people for their efforts to live out the team's values.

Make Room for Distinct Identities

When encouraging the development of strong collective identities, be sure to leave room for the expression of individual personalities as well. While it is vital for people to identify with larger groups, it is also important that they feel their contribution is in some way unique – people desire to be valued as individuals too.

A great way to encourage the expression of distinct identities is to point out people's unique contributions to their teams. Find ways to note the specific skill set that each employee brings to the team. Highlight that while one employee keeps the group laughing, another helps resolve conflicts and another notices gaps in processes.

To allow distinct identities to flourish, we should also encourage personal expression. This includes giving people the freedom to make their workspaces unique. Unfortunately, we have seen some organizations that frown upon this type of personal expression, and some even prohibit it. In our organization, one of our coworkers has Frisbees on his book shelf, another displays artwork from his children, and another shows off her favorite cartoon clippings – these things give us windows into what makes people happy. Workplaces are more interesting and inspiring when we can see the uniqueness of each team member.

Fostering Identification in Action

I, Eric, worked for a national labor organization for a number of years. The organization did an amazing job at fostering identification. Right from the start, new staff were given plenty of ways to identify with the larger group. We were given high-quality items such as clothing and work bags with the organization's branding. We were sent to a three-day-long orientation that included a review of the organization's history, its values, and its plans for the future. During orientation, we were given time and space to reflect on our own strengths, and we were encouraged to consider how we could contribute to the organization.

When the national staff gathered at various points throughout the year, there was a palpable sense of connection to each other both visually, through the branding on our clothes and work bags, and through our shared language and understanding of our history and mission. This contributed to my sense that I was part of an important team, and as a team member, I was motivated to work hard and not let my teammates down.

FACILITATE INTERDEPENDENCE

Throughout history, people have developed unique talents and strengths because such specialization is the best way for groups to ensure survival. In an organizational context, each specialist brings a unique talent to their team. Through realizing and appreciating the ways in which each person is special *and* interdependent, organizations can thrive.

In organizational culture, interdependence refers to the extent to which team members rely on each other for the functioning of their teams. Although every team is different from moment to moment, on a fundamental level, it is the interdependence of team members that makes a group of coworkers a team. As they come to realize and appreciate their interdependence, they look to each other for support in meeting objectives. Everyone contributes to the efforts of the group because they understand that the team's success is also their personal success.

Peak performing teams develop only when each member understands the link between their unique skills and the skills of others on the team. Because leaders have a unique perspective, we play a key role in developing an appreciation for interdependence among team members. Just as we must highlight the importance of the team, we should also consciously affirm that each person is needed and needs the others on the team. During team meetings and planning sessions, we can highlight the group's interdependence. And, very simply, we can encourage the expression of gratitude for the ways each person contributes by giving thanks ourselves.

Here are some ideas to help capitalize on the power of interdependence in the workplace:

Emphasize Shared Accountability

A large team project in which one person takes 100 percent of the responsibility for its failure or success has a high risk of failure because the rest of the team lacks accountability for the final product. Instead of relying on one person to be completely responsible, all team members should share collective responsibility for the outcome. When coworkers discuss success or failure while recognizing their interdependence, they are able to collectively take credit or be held accountable. This inherently builds a sense of unity and collective identity.

Members of peak performing teams are willing and able to provide feedback and support for each other because they realize that they must rely on each other for their team to function at its best. Team members should be encouraged to approach accountability conversations as *col-*

laborative conversations, asking questions like: "How are we doing as a team? How are we each doing as contributors? What kinds of support do we each need to achieve our goals?" Or, if someone has failed, "What can we all learn from this?" When team members are mutually accountable, they can check and double-check on work without hostility, ask each other questions, and take responsibility for their tasks.

Cultural and Assertive Influencers

Influencers are those who have a greater than average ability to encourage and inspire other team members. They are the people their coworkers approach for clarification and advice about how things work. Influencers play an important role in creating a positive climate for team interactions. They are not always the people who hold the highest rank on an organizational chart. In fact, they may not even be official team leaders. Often their influence is much more informal. We have noticed that there are two main types of influencers.

Cultural influencers act as ambassadors among various teams or departments. They are often (though not always) the more senior employees and leaders. They usually know the ropes and have knowledge about key aspects of the organization, including tasks and topics they are not directly responsible for. These are the people who can most fully answer the question, "How do things really work around here?" (For an example, see What a Cultural Influencer Looks Like on page 120.)

Assertive influencers, on the other hand, are those who are not afraid to confront difficult issues. They work hard and typically demonstrate long-term perseverance. Obstacles do not intimidate them, and they are able to keep working despite difficult circumstances. They are also adept at mobilizing people. Morten T. Hansen, author of *Great at Work*, calls these types of people "forceful champions" and explains that they often "make people angry about today and excited for tomorrow."[4] They do not simply work *harder*, they also work *smarter*. Assertive influencers know how to target their efforts for maximum impact. Their achievements are not temporary – they are models of sustained motivation and productivity. In our organization, Randy plays the role of assertive influencer. He has visions for the future, works with others to bring them to reality, expresses frustration when projects stall, and is never comfortable with the status quo.

It is well worth our time to identify, support, and encourage both kinds of influencers, as they have the ability to exert a positive influence on their teams. The power of their behavior is no different than the power wielded by negative individuals. Just as we ensure that we deal with difficult individuals, it is also important to highlight and capitalize on the positive influencers in our organization.

What a Cultural Influencer Looks Like

In a previous workplace, I, Wendy, quickly learned who to go to for support. The new job had many processes and procedures I needed to learn, and it was overwhelming. Thankfully, there was a woman on my team who was the "keeper of the keys." If I needed to find a form, she knew where it was. If I needed to know who could really make the final decision on a project, she could point me in the right direction. If there were stakeholders to confer with, she knew who they were. If I was unsure about union policies, she was able to clarify.

This coworker was a great source of information on the social side of things as well. She informed me that dinner club occurred on the first Friday of every month and that, if I was invited, it would be a fun way to get to know the people in my department. She quietly let me know that my winter boots should *not* go on the top shelf, as that spot was reserved for another employee who always arrived at the last minute and juggled a few personal health issues. She even knew which coffee worked best in our old coffee maker.

She was understated, always greeted everyone with a smile, and never seemed to be in a hurry. She was efficient in her role, and it quickly became clear to me that she was esteemed by her colleagues. Her understanding of the organization had breadth and depth. She became my go-to support and allowed me to quietly learn the formal and informal protocols of the workplace. Her deep understanding of the organization and her ability to connect and share that knowledge showed me the value of cultural influencers firsthand.

Showcase the Results of Collaboration

When we highlight group successes and point out the ways in which people have worked well together, we encourage individuals to look beyond their own particular roles to appreciate the contributions of their coworkers as well. These affirmations communicate that we notice and value collaboration and have a culture that cares about teamwork.

Several years ago, when we were conducting an organizational assessment of a client's company, we began the process as we normally did, but the data collection became overwhelming, and we were unsure of how to best present all the information to the client. It became clear that the job required more than the two consultants who were initially assigned to the task. After discussing the issue at a staff meeting, one employee offered to enter the data into a spreadsheet, and another offered to create a visual representation of the information, even though these tasks were outside the employees' job descriptions.

This project was spearheaded by the two consultants, but the exceptional quality of the end product was the result of a collaboration involving two additional team members. It was interesting that more collaboration led to more excitement, even though the workload had increased. We shared this story at a subsequent staff meeting and described how the project came to completion thanks to the contributions of several coworkers. Because employees felt free to move beyond their own skill sets and contribute to their coworkers' project, we saw the tangible results of teamwork.

One of our primary roles as leaders is to foster interdependence among team members. Helping our employees experience the satisfaction of team connection is vital to the long-term viability not just of individual teams, but of the organization as a whole. When employees shift their focus from individual success to team success, a crucial transformation occurs. Team members are empowered to keep each other accountable, and the quality of the work becomes the responsibility of all those involved.

SURVEY STATISTICS

I can rely on my coworkers.

According to our survey, 82 percent of people who like their workplace also feel that they can rely on their coworkers.

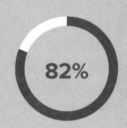

82%

DIVERSIFY YOUR TEAM

One of the keys for developing peak performing teams is to ensure that team members *think* and *operate* differently from one another. When we write that people *think* differently, we mean that it is important to have team members who process information in various different ways. For example, in our management roles at ACHIEVE, Randy is a very intuitive thinker, whereas Eric is a more logical thinker. These different ways of thinking have allowed us to more easily navigate the challenges of running our organization.

Just as people *think* differently, it is important that team members *operate* differently. By this we mean the ways people apply their unique skills in a work setting. For example, to provide our organization's services effectively, we need people who can write and speak well, but among other things, we also need others who are skilled in the area of technology. While writing and speaking are essential to the services we provide, we wouldn't communicate nearly as effectively without the technical expertise in our workplace. We have learned that the more diversity we have in how people think and operate, the more innovative and productive we are. Diversified teams allow us to perform at a higher and more sustained level.

When project teams struggle to gain momentum, and even when they fail, their lack of progress can very rarely be attributed to a single person. Rather, it can often be attributed to insufficient diversity on the team. In many cases, unproductive teams are missing the right mix of individuals required to propel the project forward. Sometimes there are too many similar people on a team, and groupthink sets in. In other situations, teams are missing one specific skill set or way of thinking.

This book is a good example of a project that required a diverse team of people to come together. It was written by four authors, and several others were instrumental in the more technical aspects of its creation. We each had a role to play in bringing our idea into reality.

Randy was the big picture person, Eric was the fine details person, Wendy was the ideas person, and Michael was the research and story person. We also relied on our internal staff: Micah tabulated and analyzed our survey data, Heidi helped manage the movement of various documents between us, and Tyler edited and formatted our manuscript. This all happened even before bringing on an additional team of talented individuals for professional editing and design.

For this book project to be a success, we needed to understand and rely on each of the unique strengths within our diversified skill set. If we as coauthors all had identical strengths, and if we hadn't had the analytical, technical, and editorial support of our internal staff, the final project would not have turned out as well. Our diversity led to a much higher quality product.

Team diversity is particularly important among leadership. As the CEO of ACHIEVE, I, Randy, am keenly aware of my weaknesses, and I have hired the other leaders in our organization with those weaknesses in mind. This can sometimes lead to strong differences of opinion when we approach certain issues and decisions. While it might have been easier to hire other leaders who simply agreed with me, ACHIEVE would not be where it is today without dissenting voices among leadership. The diversity in how each of us thinks and operates is a core strength, and we continue to perform at a high level because of it.

Peak performing teams require disruptive voices – people who challenge assumptions and provide constructive criticism of ideas. Rather than bringing a team down, criticism helps people think more critically. Critical voices push the boundaries of what our teams are capable of by helping us consider additional viewpoints. They ask the hard questions such as, "How does this actually improve things for our clients?" And they make difficult observations like, "I think we are missing the point here."

One way to guard against homogeneity is to hire for cultural diversity. People from different cultural backgrounds will often bring unique ways of thinking and relating to their teams. They may also be able to connect with a larger variety of clients or customers because of personal connections, experiences, or unique skills, such as the ability to speak multiple languages. It's important to remember that hiring for cultural diversity means more than focusing on racial or ethnic identities. It also includes aspects of identity such as ability, gender identity, sexual orientation, and other minority group identities.

Like many aspects of creating a culture where people like to work, building diversified teams requires an intentional process. Without this specific attention to diversification, we will tend to bring new people onto our teams who are "just like us," and we will miss out on opportunities for growth as a result.

Too Scared to Disagree

Unfortunately, some of our organizations are actually designed to eliminate healthy levels of dissent. When I, Michael, was in my late 20s, I started working as a human resources assistant in a large organization. In one typical meeting involving my boss, the general manager, and several others, there had been a lot of "head nodding" around the table. After the meeting, the general manager bumped into me in the hall and said: "You know, if you disagree with us, you should say so. Sometimes it's good to hear a different opinion."

My reaction was telling about the silencing power of hierarchy. I nodded my head and promptly walked away, recalling the times my boss had disagreed with the general manager only to get shut down. I thought: "There's no way I can disagree with the general manager. I'm the lowest level employee in the room."

Back then I didn't understand the importance of dissenting views. Even when the most powerful person in the room invited me to disagree, I refused to give my feedback because the group had a history and culture of rejecting contrary voices. Looking back, this taught me that diversifying a team is futile if people are not willing to disagree with others.

EMPOWER TEAMS TO MAKE DECISIONS

As leaders, we make multiple decisions every day, week, and year. Many of these decisions are best made alone. However, some leaders also assume responsibility for decisions that could be better made through the collective efforts and wisdom of a team. We have observed that failure to empower team decision making often stems from an effort to be efficient, a desire to retain control, or a lack of trust in the team. Whatever the case may be, when leaders make autonomous decisions without involving the people around them, they miss out on additional wisdom, insight, and buy-in from employees.

There are two main approaches to garnering collective wisdom: consultation and group decision making. Each has its merits as well as some pitfalls to avoid.

Consultation

If a leader prefers to retain ultimate responsibility for a decision, they can still reap some benefits of group wisdom by consulting with the team. Team members' skill sets and perspectives can complement a leader's, allowing the leader to make a well-informed decision more efficiently than if they had worked toward consensus as a group. Consultation means that the leader takes the opinions of others seriously but ultimately still has final say in the decision.

Consultation provides leaders with valuable information that can inform their decision, and it lets team members know that their voices are important and will be considered. It also communicates to team members that the final decision may not go their way. When consultation is done well, the decision maker communicates the outcome of their decision to the team along with as much rationale as possible.

We have found that people are more likely to support a decision, even if the outcome is not what they had wanted, when they feel heard *and* when their leader makes it clear that the consultation period is over. When leaders consult with their teams, they send a message that all of their voices matter. They also set a precedent for team members to consult with each other.

Two of the most common complaints we hear in our consulting work go something like this:

- "We were asked to give our opinions about which way the project should go only to find out later that the decision had already been made, and they only wanted to make us *think* our voices mattered."

- "We thought that leadership was asking *us* to make a decision, but later we discovered that they went away and made an entirely different decision that had nothing to do with our ideas."

When we hear these types of complaints, teams often also report that they feel angry, demotivated, and cynical toward leadership. So, when you are soliciting feedback, always be sure to communicate whether you are consulting or asking the group to decide. Never let a group think they are making a decision that you know you are going to make on your own.

Group Decision Making

Group decision making typically takes more time and effort than consultation. However, one of its *potential* payoffs is a high level of buy-in from those who have made the decision together. In some cases, group-made decisions can also lead to better outcomes than those made individually. We say these are *potential* payoffs because it's also possible for groups to alienate some members or conform too readily to the opinions of powerful members in the decision making process.

Group decision making can take several forms, each of which has its pros and cons. Simple majority voting is a quick and familiar way for groups to make decisions, but votes can lead to a large disaffected minority who are not happy with the results. The bar for the vote to pass can be set to a higher majority of people. However, you still risk alienating those who are in the minority.

You can also consider consensus decision making. But when doing so, ensure that team members have clarity about what consensus means. It does not typically mean that everyone is 100 percent happy with a decision. Rather, it means that all outstanding concerns with a proposal have been resolved sufficiently enough so that everybody can agree to support it.

Consensus can create incredible buy-in and support. However, it often requires more time to develop, and it becomes more difficult with larger groups. For those who are uncomfortable with a proposal, it can also create significant pressure to conform to the will of the group. For consensus decision making to work well, there must be a degree of trust and team maturity as well as a thorough understanding of the process. In addition, group members must respect their colleagues' concerns and work to resolve them rather than pressuring others to agree to a decision. (For more direction on how to make these types of decisions, see A Guide for Building Consensus on page 210 in the Resources section.)

Choosing a Process

Decision making processes shape workplace culture by indicating to team members what leaders value. For instance, consensus building emphasizes that every voice matters and that leaders will take time to ensure the workplace is inclusive and empowering. Voting shows that efficiency and majority opinion matter most. Consultation indicates that an organization values the input and wisdom of its staff. Practically, consensus is much easier in groups of fewer than 15 people. Voting works well for larger groups because it is efficient. Consultation can be used in any size group.

When you are choosing a process for yourself or your team, ask yourself these questions:

- How much does the outcome of this decision need to be supported by each person on the team?
- What might we miss if we don't involve the group in the decision?
- Are we willing to live with the results of a group decision?

The way you answer these questions will indicate the type of process you should use. (For more guidance on selecting a process, see Figure 6.1.)

When someone joins a new team, they often assume that decisions will be made in the same way that they had been on their previous teams. It is important, then, that groups are intentional about identifying how they make decisions together. At a minimum, this requires some discussion about team decision making, and it sometimes requires education about the options. Instead of making decisions without communicating about the process, be sure to outline the strategies your group will use to make decisions.

When faced with a decision, groups need to be clear about two things: the *issue* and the *process*. First, leaders should encourage teams to objectively, specifically, and clearly articulate the issue at hand. It is important to identify issues in positive ways. For example, instead of including an agenda item like, "Let's talk about our poor performance," frame it positively by saying, "Let's talk about how to reach our targets." Instead of stating, "We're frustrated by all the red tape," ask, "What can we do to streamline processes?" Second, leaders should communicate from the beginning what process will be used for each decision. This allows people to prepare and engage appropriately.

To perform at their peak, teams need decision making cultures that lead to great decisions supported by everyone affected. Like all aspects of workplace culture, team decision making requires deliberate focus and development. Mature decision making cultures help to guard against poor or unsupported decisions and the dangers of groupthink. Leaders in healthy organizational cultures work with their teams to decide which processes to use, when they will use them, and how. As new members join the team, these leaders ensure that other team members discuss the decision making culture with them.

Choosing a Process: Pros & Cons

Simple Majority Voting	Consensus Decision Making
Pros:	**Pros:**
• Efficient	• High level of buy-in
• Widely understood	• Majority of concerns are resolved
Cons:	
• Legitimate concerns may be ignored	**Cons:**
• Risk of alienating those in the minority	• May take more time
	• Difficult to reach consensus with larger groups
	• Pressure to conform

Figure 6.1

Avoid Groupthink

In 1986, NASA lost the crew of the Space Shuttle Challenger minutes after it launched. A faulty O-ring seal caused the shuttle to break apart before it left Earth's atmosphere. Investigators reported that poor decision making contributed to the accident.

NASA held to the ideal that if there were *any* questions about the safety of a launch, it was to be canceled. However, when the safety of the O-ring was brought forward by engineers prior to the launch, they were asked to reconsider their recommendation – and they did. The engineers reversed their assessment. They were influenced by their peers to reconsider their initial conclusion. The Challenger disaster is a prime and dramatic example of groupthink.[5]

Groupthink occurs when conformity to a group and its ideals is so strong that it limits critical thinking in the decision making process. Groupthink may be occurring when risks associated with a decision are downplayed or ignored or when alternative ideas are silenced. When group members do not feel safe to express their viewpoints, groupthink is likely to occur.

Groupthink can be damaging in ways that aren't immediately obvious to the group. For example, team members sometimes mistakenly believe that it is better to agree with the group than to express a contradictory opinion. We are not suggesting that teams should argue, or that all conflict is always good, but we do think that the way to get the most from our team members is to challenge opinions, consider all vantage points, wrestle with ideas, and ask hard questions. This only happens when every team member's voice is considered, not just the loudest ones.

When group harmony is valued over critical analysis, be sure to encourage all voices to speak out, especially the voices that have questions and concerns. Welcome alternative viewpoints and be thankful when people bring them forward.

CAPITALIZE ON THE POWER OF THE TEAM

While there is value in having time to ourselves, free to focus on our thoughts and tasks without distractions or interruptions from others, working alone for too long has its limitations. When we rely only on our own skills and ideas, we often fail to see problems and opportunities that might have been seen had we been working with others.

For long-term, sustained peak performance, we must come back to the group. We must rely on the collective wisdom and skills of the team to truly do exceptional work. At ACHIEVE, we have seen what can be accomplished when a group of motivated individuals works as a team – they achieve things that no one person could do on their own. This happens because people are working in a healthy workplace culture. The simple truth is: if the culture is unhealthy, your team will suffer as a result. Culture affects the team for better or for worse. Leaders must effectively develop their organization's culture in order to sustain teams that perform at their peak.

QUESTIONS FOR REFLECTION

1. What can you do to improve interdependence and identification on your team?
2. How do the members of your team *think* and *operate* differently from each other? Whose talents aren't being used as much as they could be?
3. Which people on your team are willing to disagree? How can you make it clear to everybody that dissenting opinions are valued?
4. What is your team's dominant decision making process? When would your team benefit from a different process?
5. When has groupthink been a problem in your organization?

Practice Constructive Conflict Management

MASTERING CONFLICT

For leaders, conflict can be confusing, chaotic, and unpleasant, adding pressure to our already demanding jobs. Many of us fear conflict escalation, so we either avoid conflicts or engage with them in ways that leave us regretting our actions later. However, conflict doesn't have to be destructive, it doesn't have to damage our relationships, and it doesn't have to be mysterious. The truth of the matter is that many conflicts follow a predictable path, and most of us respond to conflict in predictable ways. With this knowledge, leaders can learn how to resolve conflict constructively.

Positive experiences of working through conflict often result in renewed energy. Well managed conflict has the potential to increase our understanding of others and clarify issues that would have otherwise gone unaddressed. In fact, managing conflict effectively usually strengthens relationships.

Because conflict can so readily damage or strengthen relationships, managing it constructively is one of the key steps in creating an environment where people like to work. This chapter presents simple but powerful tools for understanding the complexities of conflict, and it contains guidance for creating a culture that doesn't fear conflict, but rather manages it effectively. It explains how conflict escalates and how you can prevent it from escalating by building a culture of trust and honest feedback. Finally, it will teach you how to prevent negative conflict triangles and empower people to have direct conversations for resolving conflict.

We use these concepts and tools in our office at ACHIEVE, and we teach them in our workshops. As organizational consultants and mediators, we help other workplaces implement these ideas. We know they are effective because we have seen them work.

SURVEY STATISTICS

Leaders in my organization work to resolve conflict quickly.

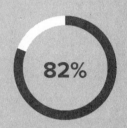

82%

According to our survey, 82 percent of people who *do not* like their workplace also don't have leaders who work to resolve conflict quickly.

THE COSTS OF POORLY MANAGED CONFLICT

Many people have experienced the impact of poorly managed conflict in the workplace. One of our survey participants noted that in their workplace, "Conflict is avoided so that the good people leave and the ones with poor boundaries and work ethics stay." Another participant reported: "Conflict is not handled well, if at all. There is great reluctance to handle difficult conversations."

Given their negative experiences with conflict, it is clear why many people find conflict to be difficult and worth avoiding. This negative view of conflict makes sense *if* we don't manage it effectively. Simmering, poorly managed, and *unresolved* conflict can be truly harmful.

In fact, the ramifications are so weighty that we devote a large portion of ACHIEVE's training and consulting services to supporting organizations that are navigating difficult conflict. We know from our consulting work and survey responses that when leaders don't work to resolve conflict quickly, morale suffers and people do not think of their workplace as a great place to work.

Interestingly, one of the strongest correlations in our survey data shows that when leaders work to resolve conflict quickly, everyone in the organization is more likely to resolve conflict constructively. (For more on this, see page 195 of the Survey Analysis.) These findings make intuitive sense. When leaders create and participate in a culture of healthy interactions, and when they assist in resolving conflict quickly, employees build positive relationships with each other as well as with leaders.

Other research has yielded more sobering facts. In one Psychometrics Canada study, more than three quarters of human resources professionals surveyed had seen conflicts result in personal insults, attacks, sickness, and absence. Eighty-one percent had seen people leave their organization as a result of conflict, and nearly half had seen someone fired because of it.[1]

When conflict is not managed well, there is a lot to lose! In our experience, poorly managed conflict has three major costs: wasted time, diminished work quality, and conflict escalation leading to structural change. Understanding these costs should motivate us to work at managing conflict effectively.

SURVEY RESPONSES

It's the *Leader's* Fault

If there's conflict on your team, there is a good chance that employees blame their leader for it. In our survey responses, a good proportion of those who told us that conflict is a problem in their organization laid the fault at their leader's feet. When we asked people what prevents their workplace from being great, they said things like this:

> "We are held back by the lack of leadership in managing conflict."
> "Our leadership team needs improvement in dealing with conflict."

"The lack of follow-through from leadership when dealing with conflict among employees is frustrating."

Some survey participants said their leaders address conflict, but too slowly, while others said their leaders are conflict avoiders:

"Managers leave things to fester with no meaningful intervention."
"They are much happier shifting the blame instead of dealing with it."
"Supervisors just hope the conflict will go away."

One person blamed leadership for *not knowing* about conflicts, writing, "At times management isn't aware of some of the conflict/issues that are going on, and I feel they should be more perceptive of this."

Whether or not leaders feel equipped to respond to workplace conflict is beside the point because, as our survey demonstrates, employees expect that leaders will be proactive and play a supportive role. Although their levels of direct involvement will vary, leaders will always have a role in managing conflict because they contribute to the overall culture in which conflict is resolved. Their support, or lack thereof, is sure to have an impact.

Wasted Time

When we give time and attention to conflict without managing it effectively, it means we are not giving that time to our work. Unresolved or poorly managed conflict takes up an enormous amount of mental energy. We spend time rehashing what has happened and looking for a way to end the conflict and bring things back into balance. Our attention shifts from our work to our conflict.

Poorly managed conflict wastes the time not only of those directly involved, but of those on the periphery as well. As leaders, we spend valuable time and energy dealing with unhealthy conflict among employees. In turn, employees spend time discussing conflict around the water cooler. Over time, more and more people are drawn into the conversations, even if they were not involved to begin with.

The average US employee spends 2.8 hours per week dealing with conflict, according to a major survey conducted by CPP, Inc.[2] If an employee makes $21 per hour, they are getting paid over $3,000 each year just to deal with conflict – and this doesn't even account for the indirect costs mentioned in this chapter.

Diminished Work Quality

Employees make sound decisions when they feel free to speak their mind, when they trust others to give them constructive feedback, and when they are working collaboratively. But under the pressure of unhealthy conflict, innovation, creativity, and the motivation to produce high-quality work wane.

If we manage conflict poorly, people may begin to act in aggressive and retaliatory ways. As conflict escalates, they may begin to sabotage work projects to get back at others. They might take out their frustrations by withholding information or helpful advice, and in extreme cases, they may even damage physical property such as tools or business supplies.

In one memorable situation, a group of employees in an organization we were working with openly shared that they were planning to verbally attack the "other side" during an upcoming staff meeting, and they planned strategies for defending themselves from a counterattack. Yet this same group expressed frustration that they couldn't properly focus on their work as a result of the open and hostile conflict.

Conflict Escalation and Structural Change

Unfortunately, when conflict is handled poorly, open attacks and defensive posturing are probable outcomes. Most conflict resolution researchers and practitioners believe that conflict escalates in predictable and increasingly damaging ways if it is not addressed skillfully and appropriately. We have found this to be true in our own work as well.

We are indebted to the lifelong work, research, and writing of John

Paul Lederach in particular, who has significantly shaped the way we understand conflict escalation and conflict transformation. Lederach has worked with seemingly intractable conflicts involving multiple stakeholders in situations of serious violence, as well as with organizational and interpersonal conflict. He believes, "Conflict is normal in human relationships, and conflict is a motor of change."[3] Lederach has observed that conflicts follow predictable patterns whether they are interpersonal, organizational, or societal.

There are various perspectives about the exact number and nature of stages in conflict escalation. But most practitioners agree that the beginning point in any conflict is usually not inherently bad. However, as conflict escalates, it becomes harder and harder to resolve productively. When conflicts aren't resolved productively, they can often end by changing the structure of organizations or relationships.

We've outlined five levels of conflict escalation below, each with an increasing level of complexity (see Figure 7.1). Notice how the original issue changes or gets lost as the level of complexity increases.

Conflict Escalation

Level 1: Problem Identification
Focus: disagreement, misunderstanding, perceived injustice
Action: we *talk with* the other person

Level 2: Fundamental Attribution Error
Focus: character or culture as the problem
Action: we *talk less* to the other person

Level 3: Alliance Building
Focus: aligning with others who share our view
Action: we *talk about* the other person and their side

Level 4: Open Confrontation
Focus: open hostility
Action: we *fight with* the other side

Level 5: Structural Change
Focus: dividing relationships or organizations
Action: we *no longer talk*

Figure 7.1

At Level 1, conflict begins when we identify a problem that needs to be resolved, experience a misunderstanding, or perceive an injustice. Assuming that the relationship has been okay up to this point, we can normally resolve the issue through conversations or simple actions. However, if we are not able to resolve the matter easily or to our satisfaction, we usually move to Level 2.

At Level 2, we begin to believe that the conflict has to do with the *character* of the other person. This is because of a bias in our thinking called the Fundamental Attribution Error (FAE). The FAE causes us to overlook the circumstances that may have played a role in the person's actions and judge them based on who we perceive them to be personally. For example, if someone's actions are perceived as "bad" at Level 1, by Level 2 we assume they must be a "bad" person.

Because we are biased in our judgment of the person on the other side of the conflict, we start to notice other things we don't like about them. We see more and more of their actions as aspects of their flawed character. Unfortunately, in all likelihood they are also committing the FAE. They believe that *our* character is lacking and that we are the problem. If we are unable to take a step back from our thinking errors at Level 2, our conflict will inevitably escalate to Level 3.

At Level 3, we take steps to protect ourselves and bolster our cause by building alliances with others who think like us. We stop talking with the other side about the issues. Instead, we talk about the situation with people who we think will support us. We may turn to our friends, our leaders, the human resources department, or the person who sits nearest to us in the office. Unfortunately, as we build our alliances, so does the other side. As more and more people get drawn in, our conflict becomes increasingly complicated. As our alliances form and our groups develop identities around their views of the conflict, we prepare to defend ourselves and to fight. When this happens, we move to Level 4.

At Level 4, we look for ways to "win," or ways to shut down the other side. This inevitably results in confrontation and public hostility. The group we mentioned in an earlier example, which was planning their attack for the next staff meeting, was at Level 4. Once we reach this stage, we are so entrenched in our experience of the conflict and our views of the other person or side are so rigid that we are only one step away from making a change in our relational structure.

At Level 5, communication becomes so difficult that we are often forced to find a way to change our relational structure, usually through some act of force or flight. In a marriage, the change may be separation or divorce. In an interpersonal workplace conflict, one colleague might get moved to another department, quit, or get fired. At broader levels, departments are reorganized, companies divide, religious organizations split, and where there was once one nation, there are now two or more.

It Got Ugly Quickly

Early in my career, I, Wendy, worked at an organization where I observed a Level 1 conflict as it escalated all the way to Level 5. In my workplace, there were two individuals who were both skilled and committed to their work. However, they were also both very headstrong.

At one staff meeting, management announced that the organization had received some additional funding. The staff were thrilled, but they then had to decide how the money would be allocated. In the following discussion, two staff members voiced very different opinions about how to best use the funding. The meeting became tense, they raised their voices, and arguments ensued.

It was only after the dispute had escalated and several personal accusations had been uttered that the manager finally interjected. After the meeting, the incident was not addressed, and both people began ignoring each other and talking behind the other's back. They each talked to me and other staff members in an attempt to try to get us "on their side."

A few months later, one of the individuals involved resigned. The conflict had taken a toll on her personal life, and she was no longer able to do her job well, so she decided that her best option was a Level 5 structural change – quitting her job. Our organization lost a valuable employee because of poorly managed conflict.

Although this progression through the five levels of conflict didn't happen overnight, it did happen quickly. I often wonder what would have happened if the senior leader had stepped in during that first meeting and helped the individuals focus on the good problem that we all shared rather than allowing them to begin attacking each other. My sense is that the conflict could have been addressed in a healthy way for both the individuals and the organization as a whole.

TRANSFORMING CONFLICT

While we believe that some relationships and structures need to be changed or ended, we do not believe this always has to come about through an unhealthy process of conflict escalation. Our goal should not be to prevent conflict at all costs, but rather to manage conflict proactively, transform negative conflict, address issues as they arise, and embrace the opportunities that conflict brings. In order to create such a culture, we suggest that you use the following strategies, which we discuss in greater detail throughout this chapter:

- Train staff and leaders in conflict resolution and coaching skills.
- Build a culture of trust.
- Incorporate honest mutual feedback.
- Prevent conflict triangles.
- Know when to use conflict management specialists.

PROVIDE CONFLICT RESOLUTION TRAINING

At ACHIEVE, we are often asked to provide mediation work for organizations. In the course of our engagement with these organizations, we frequently provide conflict resolution skills training. We have discovered through feedback from our clients that, although mediation work is helpful for dealing with significant issues, the training we provide is vital over the long term as it builds the staff's capacity to work through matters on their own before conflicts escalate to higher levels.

To create a culture that embraces and transforms conflict, we suggest providing conflict resolution skills training for the whole organization. We know that training staff in conflict resolution skills is one of the most effective ways to prevent the negative spiral through the five stages of conflict escalation. Training teaches strategies for resolving conflict through direct discussion and other conflict resolution skills, and it alerts people to potential thinking errors such as the FAE.

With training, people more frequently resolve conflict at Level 1. When they find themselves slipping into Level 2 thinking errors, training can help them trigger different thinking processes, which causes them to engage differently and deal with most matters effectively through direct discussion.

At Level 3, when people feel stuck in their conflict and need another person's help, use conflict resolution coaching rather than letting alliances form. Conflict resolution coaching is focused conversation built upon the belief that people will be most satisfied with the resolution to a conflict when they have a direct hand in shaping that resolution.

Coaching helps people think through their options, plan their conversations, and build skills for working through conflict. It helps them consider where they may be wrong or how they may have contributed to the situation. In the words of The Arbinger Institute's *The Anatomy of Peace*, "No conflict can be solved so long as all parties are convinced they are right. Solution is possible only when at least one party begins to consider how [they] might be wrong."[4] Coaching enables people to identify their own thinking errors and engage directly with each other in new and different ways. Leaders and staff can be trained in coaching skills through workshops and other learning programs, or organizations can hire external consultants for conflict resolution coaching.

If people are still not able to transform conflict on their own or with the benefit of coaching, consider engaging conflict management specialists for assistance. Conflict management specialists can provide clear processes for handling conflict, and they can mediate conversations between the people involved. This allows everyone to make decisions together about how to manage their conflict, including whether they need to change the ways they relate or, sometimes, end their relationships. This gives people the best chance for achieving positive resolutions and leaving their dignity intact. (For a practical guide to managing conflict, see the Conflict Transformation Guide on page 212 in the Resources section.)

BUILD A CULTURE OF TRUST

Through our work as mediators, we have come to see that mutual trust is a prerequisite for healthy conflict management. When those involved in conflict refuse to participate in mediation with each other, trust is the most frequently cited reason. They either don't trust the process or they don't trust that the other party will respect them, behave well during the mediation, or follow through on their commitments. Without trust, people refuse to engage in conflict resolution even with a professional mediator present.

Trust means that a person can discuss what really matters to them without significant fear that someone else will use that information against them or judge them negatively for what they are saying. It also means that people believe others on their team will act with good intentions. Trust is built through relationships and must be anchored in a healthy understanding of each person in the relationship. Trust is also built by using constructive processes for addressing conflict.

In a workplace where team members do not openly express their thoughts out of a fear of conflict, mediocre decisions are often the result. When we experience an absence of trust, we waste huge amounts of time and energy investing ourselves in defensive or protective behaviors. We are also reluctant to ask for help or assist each other.

To avoid such a scenario, we need everyone within our workplace to understand that conflict can actually be helpful when it is built on a bedrock of trust. To put it another way, in order for our teams to engage in positive conflict that leads to better workplace resolutions, we must first trust each other and our processes.

One significant conflict we mediated involved a department in a very large organization. A new manager had come into the department with a mandate to make changes, but staff had little to no relationship with her. As a result, the new manager's decisions were met with suspicion and even outrage.

When staff challenged the new manager's decisions, she responded with defensiveness, and the conflict quickly escalated. The department as a whole did not *trust* the manager, and the manager didn't trust the staff. The only way forward for this group was to begin to build relationships with each other so that they could develop trust and learn to engage in positive conflict resolution.

Developing trusting relationships is hard work, and it involves some risk. It's often difficult for people to be honest for fear of being judged by others. And yet it's only when people are vulnerable that strong relationships can be built. Given the risk that some people feel when sharing details about themselves, we encourage leaders to take the first step and model openness.

In our own organization, and when we are leading other groups, one of the ways we build trusting relationships is by leading discussions that help people understand the experiences that have shaped the ways their coworkers think and act. For instance, during team development events, we may ask people to share something that has been significant in their life outside of work in the past year, or we may have them share a story from their childhood. We also use simple personality tools like the "ACHIEVE Personality Dimensions Assessment" (described on page 44) to help staff learn and appreciate each other's preferences and tendencies.[5]

Given that power is structured by rank in most organizations, leaders must learn to lead by example to create a culture that is not afraid of conflict. Our willingness to share openly as leaders will show employees that it is safe for them to voice their opinions as well. We must also acknowledge and validate others who risk sharing openly.

If we have the courage to share with openness, we communicate to staff that they are safe to share as well. When we build relationships through sharing who we are and caring for others, we model behavior for others to follow. When we invite others to disagree, listen to their concerns, and apologize for our mistakes, we show that it is safe for others to do the same.

As leaders, we must create a culture of trust so that our employees can truly express what they are thinking and feeling when conflict occurs. When our workplaces are safe and people feel that their opinions are heard, they will support decisions more readily even if the outcomes aren't exactly what they had wanted. This results in superior decision making and organizational outcomes. It builds a culture where people bring their best to the table. (For more resources on building a culture of trust, see our Conflict Management & Respectful Workplace Guidelines, on page 213 in the Resources section.)

TRUST AND HONEST MUTUAL FEEDBACK

To effectively build a trusting culture where conflict is dealt with in healthy and constructive ways, everyone within an organization must be able to give and receive honest and mutual feedback. In addition to building trust through relationships, our team members should also be aware of some of the natural inclinations that can prevent them from giving or receiving honest feedback. For example, some people do not normally provide any *direct* feedback. Rather than risking a negative confrontation, they try to "let it go." This often leads to a buildup of resentment or an eventual blow up. Other people are more than willing to offer feedback, but they get defensive whenever anybody gives feedback to them. Both responses get in the way of honest and mutual feedback.

In order to engage in honest and mutual feedback, we need practices that move beyond our normal relational patterns. Creating such a culture takes effort and leadership, but the payoff is a motivated, self-managing, and continuously improving team. Here are four important steps for creating such a culture:

Unite the Team Around Purpose and Values

When feedback is anchored in a commonly held purpose and set of organizational values, employees are less likely to grow defensive because they believe the feedback will help them achieve the goals they share with the organization.

The simplest way to get people to identify with your organization's purpose and values is to involve team members in their development (as discussed in Chapter 2). When this is not possible, regularly communicate your purpose and values and discuss what they mean in terms of behavior.

Feedback is more relatable and productive when it references shared vision and values. For instance, at ACHIEVE one of our goals is to surprise and delight our clients when we can. When a colleague asks for feedback about their work with one of our clients, any one of us can easily ask, "How does your approach fit with our goal of surprising and delighting clients when we can?" Asking this question provides us with a reference point for evaluating actions, which is grounded in our goals and values.

As consultants we have also led other teams in creating their own feedback guidelines. An agreement will often contain elements such as these:

- We commit to anchoring our feedback in our values, purpose, and goals.
- We commit to being honest about our assessment of each other's work, not overstating problems or attacking other people.
- We commit to taking criticism of our work not as a personal attack but as an opportunity for self-improvement.
- We commit to being just as candid during meetings as we are in the break room.
- We commit to regularly checking in regarding the quality of our relationships with each other.

Honest and mutual feedback fosters a culture of adaptability. Including it as an aspect of your values or purpose primes those in your organization to view feedback as helpful rather than as fodder for conflict.

Increase Connection Time

The following incredibly powerful fact about human relationships is also one of the simplest: face-to-face meetings, retreats, conferences, meals, and coffee breaks together build our trust in each other and increase our fluency in providing honest and mutual feedback.

Without sufficient connection time, we are likely to see damaging behaviors like this one described by a survey participant: "Leaders do not always solve conflicts in a personal manner. They send emails rather than speaking to people." Actions such as this drive disconnection and are not likely to help staff address conflict.

Set the Tone for Honest Feedback

In addition to modeling vulnerability, we must demonstrate the value of honest and mutual feedback by inviting it from coworkers of all ranks. When we respond to feedback with gratitude and curiosity, others open up to doing the same. By contrast, if we don't invite feedback, or if we respond to it defensively, we hamper our own growth, send chills through the organization, and ultimately create barriers to the organization's success.

If you do not regularly receive feedback that challenges your assumptions or opinions, it could mean that people are not comfortable sharing what they really think. Healthy disagreement helps to ensure that our organization is on the right track and making good decisions.

At ACHIEVE, we encourage staff to share their ideas and voice their opinions – especially when they disagree with us as leaders. We welcome additional perspectives, and we are careful not to shut down staff when they are courageous enough to bring forward new ideas. This can happen in meetings or one-on-one. We recently met with a newer member of our team who had demonstrated high potential, and we invited him to challenge us as leaders more than he had been. While this direction was surprising to him, after deeper conversation we could tell that it was also an empowering invitation.

Focus on Issues, Not People

As humans, we're not wired well for day-to-day organizational conflict. Our typical responses are to look for an escape route away from the danger (flight), to ignore or hide from it (freeze), or to respond with retaliation (fight). None of these natural responses are helpful in the workplace. Moving constructively through conflict requires us to stick with uncomfortable situations without letting our tendency for self-preservation kick in. In order to persist through discomfort, we need to know that we are not being attacked.

If we are going to engage in conflict or honest and mutual feedback productively, we need to know that our character will not be maligned. To put it positively, we need others to believe the best about us and demonstrate curiosity about our behaviors that may not make sense to them.

For leaders, one of the most helpful strategies for minimizing the sense of danger, and its associated flight, freeze, and fight responses, is to keep everyone focused on the *issues* that need to be resolved rather than on what they think about the *people* involved. Very simply, this means focusing on observable data, such as what someone did or said, rather than judgments about their intent or character.

For example, instead of saying something like, "When you tried to shut that customer down…" you could say, "When you started speaking while the customer was speaking…" Instead of saying, "You are lazy," you could say, "I noticed that others offered assistance during the meeting, but I did not hear the same from you." Notice how the first statement in each example contains interpretation or judgment of someone's intent or character, while the second statements do not. Consequently, the first statements will likely provoke more defensiveness from the listener than the second ones. It's much easier to discuss someone's actions, which are changeable, rather than their character, which is not as changeable.

Creating a culture of honest and mutual feedback is a challenging but worthwhile task. When employees feel comfortable enough to practice feedback, they forge stronger relationships, improve their collective work performance, and reduce negative conflict.

PREVENT CONFLICT TRIANGLES

Conflict destabilizes relationships. In an effort to stabilize their relationships, those in conflict often seek out the help of a third person for support. In a workplace, the third person is frequently a trusted leader. This usually creates a conflict triangle (see Figure 7.2).

The Conflict Triangle

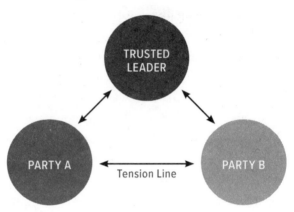

Figure 7.2

Imagine that two colleagues, Jim and Carly, are having a heated argument. Jim feels fed up and walks into his manager's office. He begins by saying something like this: "You wouldn't believe what a dumb thing Carly did today! We were discussing the new proposal when…" The story goes on from there, but a conflict triangle is already beginning to form. The manager is already evaluating the situation based on her prior experiences with both employees and the story Jim is telling. She might be privately siding with either Jim or Carly or wishing she could just ignore the issue altogether. No matter what she feels or thinks, the manager is no longer neutral.

A common dynamic is unfolding within this story – one that involves victims, villains, and allies. The manager already knows the name of the *villain* (Carly) and the *victim* (Jim) in this story – at least according to Jim, who believes that Carly is in the wrong. As the listener, the manager is starting to play another familiar role – that of the *ally*. We call this relational drama "The Age Old Story."

The Age Old Story

As leaders, it's very easy to become caught up in the stories staff tell us about their colleagues. After all, relational drama is captivating. But getting caught up in the drama tends to produce poor results in relationships. It doesn't help us resolve conflict and it distracts everyone from their work.

When people describe their conflicts, they tend to follow a very familiar storyline that goes something like this:

> I was being a reasonable person with good intentions (innocent victim), when – BAM! – out of nowhere, another person (guilty villain) did a bad thing to me. It's not fair! I want you (heroic ally) to side with me and help me out of this mess.

We can find this storyline in many, many places: fairy tales, romantic comedies, action movies, Disney movies, and even some sacred stories. In fact, The Age Old Story is so pervasive that we easily slip into its roles without questioning whether they are accurate or helpful in our particular situation.

And therein lies a major problem: The Age Old Story provides us with scripts for how to think and behave within what Stephen B. Karpman calls The Drama Triangle. Karpman conceived of The Drama Triangle in 1968 to map the relationships among people in conflict. He described the roles as the "victim," the "rescuer," and the "persecutor."[6] We have adapted The Drama Triangle to fit with our understanding of conflict, and we therefore use the terms "innocent victim," "heroic ally," and "guilty villain."

The Drama Triangle

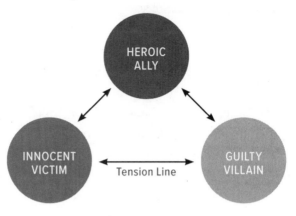

Figure 7.3

To challenge this dynamic, we need to begin by understanding that falling into The Age Old Story reduces everyone's capacity to solve problems and grow as human beings. Unlike listening to fairy tales or watching movies, in real life we usually have the power to shape our futures and create new, richer, and more accurate stories.

So what can we do to reduce the drama when someone begins telling The Age Old Story? To break out of the script, we must first be aware of two major pitfalls.

The first pitfall is silence or inaction in response to the story. Doing nothing is a type of action that may be interpreted by the storyteller as, "The leader doesn't care." In our example, inaction from the manager would likely cause Jim to view her as a villain and seek out another ally instead.

The second pitfall occurs when the leader takes up the storyteller's cause. If the manager sides with Jim and takes up the role of heroic ally, Carly will view her as a villain, and Jim will view her as an ally. Jim will also expect her to act like an ally – to either take up the fight with him or bring justice to the villain.

Workplace conflicts in real life usually don't have fully innocent victims or fully guilty villains. Rather, each person has usually acted in ways that seemed reasonable to them given their circumstances. In claiming their innocence, the victim normally commits a Fundamental Attribution Error by judging the *character* of the other person as "bad" while seeing their own *behavior* as reasonable – not even questioning their own character.

As leaders, when we side with one person over the other, we create divisive politics within the organization. Instead of siding with one person or playing the role of heroic ally, we need to empower others to solve their own problems. We must help the "storytellers" imagine different stories that empower them to act in self-supporting ways. And we must always keep people focused on the issues rather than on matters of character.

How to Change the Story

Don't let yourself buy into The Age Old Story. Rather than staying silent or following these scripted roles, you must commit to *changing* the stories. Begin by listening and showing care. You can do this with a simple response such as: "Thanks for talking to me about this. I can see that this matters to you."

As you begin to address the issues within the story, remember that the storyteller will probably describe their own good intentions and try to minimize their negative impact. This is entirely normal. However, if you are going to provide a helpful response, realize that the stark contrast between their innocent victim mentality and their casting of the other person as guilty villain is often exaggerated.

In addition, keep in mind that you don't have to be the heroic ally. You can reduce the drama by helping your colleague consider creating a different story. Begin with simple questions that allow the storyteller to consciously move away from The Age Old Story script toward a more empowering one that will ultimately reduce the resentment, hostility, and lack of trust (see Figure 7.4).

In most cases, The Age Old Story is inaccurate and disempowering. The storyteller is rarely an innocent victim who is powerless to act in self-supporting ways. Someone who has been cast as a guilty villain is rarely purely malicious. You don't have to be the heroic ally, but rather you can be someone who can help your colleague tell a new, more empowering story.

While the concepts we have reviewed in this section are true in many cases, it is important to note that there can be true victims in our workplaces. This happens in situations of bullying, harassment, and violence. In those cases, leaders need to take steps to shield victims from further harm and hold the people that have harmed them accountable.

Questions to Change Stories

What if the other person wasn't trying to be hurtful?
- What if their intention was entirely different?
- What if they are feeling as though they have been hurt?
- How could you ask them about their thoughts?

What power do you have to change what is happening?
- What might you be able to do to make things come out more positively?
- How might you invite the other person into a new way of working together?

What do you want to do next?
- What resources do you have to assist you?
- What further supports do you need?

Figure 7.4

The Age Old Story Among Friends

The Age Old Story can be enacted in both our work and our personal relationships. Its power to shape our thinking and actions is the same regardless of the context we find ourselves in.

I, Michael, am friends with a couple that is separating. They are caught in The Age Old Story, each convinced that they are the victim and the other is the villain. Sure enough, they have each asked me to be the heroic ally by saying things like, "Tell him that he should..." and "Tell her she's got to..." Perhaps the strangest part of this situation is that, at one point, I was tempted to play along. They both wanted me to be their heroic ally, and a part of me really did want to fill that role!

However, I know that this wouldn't actually have been productive – I wouldn't have been able to fix their relationship. But they still wanted me to help fix it, and my attempts at helping them to understand each other were failing. One day, while having coffee with one of them, I said something like this: "I appreciate you sharing all this with me. I really want to help you guys. But I'm going to ask you to stop trying to get me to work out issues that, in the years you were married, you didn't work out with each other. Whether separated or not, it's your relationship, and I'm not able to help you fix it." By breaking out of The Age Old Story myself, I could, with integrity, invite them to do the same.

This enabled me to ask the kind of questions I would have asked if I were their mediator, such as, "What if that's not what she meant?" While this didn't save their marriage (it was 10 years too late for that), it did prevent me from getting caught in The Age Old Story of my friends.

While responding to my friends' situation in this way was not particularly easy, it was freeing. It allowed us to relate on an equal footing again because I didn't have to be the heroic ally and neither of them had to be the villain.

USE CONFLICT MANAGEMENT SPECIALISTS

Conflict transformation is hard work that requires skill, patience, and resources. Most leaders have not been trained in conflict resolution skills, let alone in coaching for conflict resolution or mediation. In some cases, conflicts brew for months or years before a leader even becomes aware there is a problem. Given these dynamics, many leaders legitimately struggle with knowing what to do about conflict and how to resolve it.

Before hiring a specialist, we suggest trying informal coaching for conflict resolution. Use the principles contained in the preceding section on The Age Old Story to do this. If informal coaching doesn't work, consider bringing in a trained resource person for assistance. The world is full of professional conflict management specialists who can assist in a number of ways. Although larger organizations may already have internal staff members who are trained in conflict resolution coaching and mediation, both internal and external specialists have their benefits (see Figure 7.5).

A good conflict management consultant will help you decide which approach is best for your team. In some cases, they may offer basic conflict resolution skills training, which will provide a foundation for effective conversations. In other situations, they may recommend specialized coaching for conflict resolution or mediation for the parties involved. Depending on the complexity of the situation, any combination of these strategies or other group processes could be used.

As mediators and consultants ourselves, we also believe that whatever a conflict management specialist does, they need to help the organization's leadership develop a plan to continue supporting the parties involved. Ultimately, long-term direction for dealing with conflict needs to come from within the organization itself.

Choosing a Specialist

Advantages of an Inside Specialist	Advantages of an Outside Specialist
• Knows the organizational context • May already have the trust of the parties • Usually requires minimal additional cost • Can keep organizational values front and center	• Perceived as fully unbiased • Typically highly trained • Adheres to professional standards • Is cheaper than litigation

Figure 7.5

The Benefits of Conflict Management

We were pleasantly surprised by some of the healthy ways our survey participants' organizations deal with conflict. In their responses, people shared simple and powerful nuggets of wisdom for dealing with conflict. They wrote about dealing with it quickly and constructively:

> "Conflicts are resolved openly and promptly."
> "When a disagreement occurs, people immediately address it in a professional and constructive manner."

Survey participants also told us what they like about *how* conflict is resolved. When describing strategies for dealing with conflict, they made statements like these:

> "We own our mistakes, apologize, and ask for help if needed."
> "We *don't* make assumptions but instead ask questions."
> "We keep in close communication with each other."

Participants who work in organizations where conflict is managed well often wrote positively about the role of leadership:

> "My leader is doing all she can to resolve conflicts within our office."
> "We can bring a conflict to our supervisor or manager, and they give us the support we need to resolve it."
> "Our leaders are great role models."

We see a simple and profound pattern in these responses that provides a road map for creating a culture where conflict is handled in healthy ways. It goes like this:

1. Conflicts should be resolved immediately, openly, and constructively.
2. Each person should own their mistakes and ask questions rather than making assumptions.
3. Leaders should support employees to directly resolve their conflicts.

When organizations follow this three-part formula, they will be well on their way to creating and sustaining a healthy organizational culture.

CONFLICT & ORGANIZATIONAL CULTURE

We know that creating a culture of constructive conflict management is a key aspect of creating a workplace where people like to work. People are less stressed and anxious about conflict when they feel safe in their workplace, know that they can address conflict in a positive way, and trust leadership to step in when needed. When conflict is well managed, people feel like they can address issues as they arise, they are comfortable giving and receiving feedback, and they ultimately develop trust in each other. When conflict isn't managed well, negativity permeates the workplace.

The tools and practices in this chapter have proven themselves to us and the people we work with as effective for creating a workplace culture characterized by constructive conflict management. Addressing conflict well is an essential component in building vibrant workplace cultures. It will not only create workplaces where people like to be, it will also help you reach your organizational goals and accomplish your mission.

QUESTIONS FOR REFLECTION

1. How far do conflicts usually escalate before they are dealt with? Who deals with them and how?
2. How do you show your team that you trust them? What steps could your team take to improve trust?
3. How well does your organization practice honest and mutual feedback? How can your leadership team be more deliberate in setting a tone that welcomes feedback?
4. Think of a time when you heard someone telling The Age Old Story in your workplace. How did this narrative shape the actions people took in response to the conflict?
5. What is your organization's approach to conflict management? How conscious and overt is it? How could it be strengthened?

How to Change Culture

WHEN TO CHANGE CULTURE

If you experience unhealthy culture on a daily basis, or if you witness things like cynicism, distrust, or overly aggressive behavior in your workplace, it's time to do something about it. When your culture is okay but not great – when it's not so much dysfunctional as it is just missing a little something – you should also act to improve it. If your culture is great, remember that it's always evolving and, like a garden, will still require tending over time.

According to the Deloitte "Global Human Capital Trends Report," out of more than seven thousand CEOs and human resources leaders surveyed, only 19 percent felt they had the "right culture."[1] This means that for the majority of organizations, a culture change is needed.

Changing culture is difficult because in most cases it has developed over many years and has become deeply ingrained in the organization. Some leaders haven't even considered whether their organizational culture is healthy or unhealthy – they feel that, "This is just how things work around here." Like fish in water, people are simply immersed in the culture around them and rarely stop to ponder it. Regardless of how unhealthy a culture is, people tend to get comfortable living within it, so making even incremental changes can feel as challenging as swimming against a current.

Through our consulting experiences, we have seen that leaders usually don't consider working on their culture until something bad happens. Unfortunately, it often takes exceptionally negative experiences such as a financial crisis or the loss of key employees for leaders to think about organizational culture.

Regardless of an organization's struggles, change will not occur until leaders recognize that the status quo is unacceptable. And even then, change won't be easy. By its very nature, organizational culture change is challenging, time consuming, and sometimes painful. In his book *The Culture Engine*, S. Chris Edmonds writes: "Culture change, or if you prefer, culture refinement, is not something to be taken casually. It must be seen as vital work that needs time, energy, and intention."[2]

In this final chapter, we look more closely at the culture change process and provide a framework for changing workplace culture. We'll look at how to build a team to lead the culture change process and then focus on the four phases of the culture change cycle. This chapter concludes with our thoughts about sustaining changes over time.

THE CULTURE CHANGE TEAM

In order to successfully change your culture, you first need a committed group of people who will lead the change. Without at least a small group of dedicated culture change leaders, it's hard to even begin. The good news is that it only takes a few dedicated and persistent people to make a powerful impact within your organization.

For culture transformation to be successful, senior leaders need to be among the driving forces for change, as others will normally take cues from them. But it's also important to include a cross section of your workforce on the culture change team. This should include managers as well as lower-level employees who have bought into the vision for change and have the ability to influence others. The team should include *cultural influencers* as well as *assertive influencers,* as they are the people who can naturally propel change (see page 119).

The following questions offer a guide for building your team:

- Who among senior leadership needs to be on the team because efforts for change are likely to stall without them?
- Who among our staff are passionate about seeing change?
- Who are the cultural influencers who will naturally inspire others and bring them along with the change process?
- Who are the assertive influencers who will keep our process moving forward?
- Who will we include in order to have diverse viewpoints on the team?

Once the culture change team has been created, formalizing and recognizing the team helps to build credibility and clarity for the change process. One way to do this is to name the group in a way that clearly identifies who the people are who are leading the efforts of culture change. Something as simple as "The Culture Change Team" will suffice.

To provide additional credibility for the team, it is helpful to explain to staff why the change process has been initiated, how the team has been chosen, and what they are tasked with doing. In particular, emphasize the opportunity for positive growth rather than the dysfunction in the current culture.

The size of your culture change team could vary based on the overall size of your organization and the variety of voices you wish to include. From a functional perspective, we have found that teams of five to seven people work best. Resist the temptation to create a large team. Instead, periodically bring in a consultant or someone new from within your organization when you need an additional perspective.

MAKE SMALL & SIMPLE CHANGES *NOW*

An overarching principle to keep in mind throughout the change process is that if you see something that could be easily changed, you should change it *now*. This allows you to capitalize on quick wins to build momentum.

For example, an archaic and punitive policy around the use of vacation time can be quickly rewritten, and the new policy can be implemented. A side lunch room that had been reserved for senior leadership could have a wall removed so that it becomes a part of the larger lunch room. Although this may be costlier than writing a policy, it can still be done with relatively little effort.

One leader we interviewed told us that he improved his farm's work culture by putting a refrigerator full of snacks, fruit, and drinks in the main office. The result was an increase in staff morale. Because of this one simple change, early morning coffees, lunch meetings, and end-of-day conversations happened more organically and more frequently.

Make small and simple changes at every point throughout the process. For many changes, you don't have to wait to gather more information from focus groups and reports. This principle allows you to achieve some early wins to show that success is possible. Some barriers to healthy culture may be eliminated immediately, and changing them quickly builds momentum for the longer-term changes.

A PROCESS FOR CULTURE CHANGE

Given how difficult it is to change culture, organizations must be intentional and focused when attempting change. To help organizations change culture, we have developed a framework involving four phases. We explore these phases in more detail throughout the remainder of this chapter:

- **Phase 1: Assess your current culture.** Clarity about the present situation allows you to more easily plan for change. Talk with and listen to everyone in your organization. Consider your current strengths, as well as the aspects of your culture that are holding you back.
- **Phase 2: Envision a desired culture.** What would your ideal culture look like? What elements would be added, and what

aspects of your current culture would you remove? Be sure to invite everyone to contribute to this process – employees and leaders alike.

- **Phase 3: Share and teach the culture.** Once you have defined what a better culture might look like, share your vision widely. Start showing people what the future will be like once the change has been made. Provide training for the behaviors that are needed for the new culture to thrive.
- **Phase 4: Monitor and provide accountability.** Changes to workplace culture are usually fragile at first, so monitor the changes, check in with employees, and offer coaching. Pay attention to signs that people are reverting to past behaviors, and address these issues quickly.

All culture change requires some version of these phases. Lasting change usually takes a considerable length of time, so be prepared to invest a substantial amount of energy into the process. While the process we define is fluid, skipping aspects of the phases only creates the perception that things are happening more quickly than they actually are and will typically hamper your efforts. (A user-friendly guide for working through these four phases can be found in the Culture Change Guide, on page 217 in the Resources section.)

These four phases can be thought of as a cycle for continually improving your organization's culture (see Figure 8.1). As you move through the cycle, each phase connects to and interacts with the next. It's important to note that you should always be somewhere in the cycle. Even if you have a healthy culture, you should be monitoring it – you will never be completely finished.

The Continuous Improvement Cycle

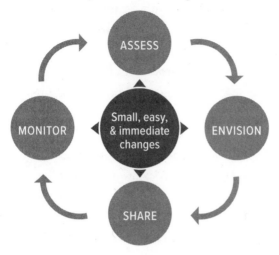

Figure 8.1

PHASE 1: ASSESS YOUR CURRENT CULTURE

To change your organization's culture, you must first truly understand its current culture. Only when you have a clear picture of who you are *now* can you decide who you'd like to be in the future.

Take some time to observe your culture as if you were an outsider. How do staff interact with clients? How are conflicts resolved – or not? How do managers relate to employees? How do employees relate to each other? Do you notice tension, discomfort, or laughter? Look for things that are *not* there as well – are conversations or processes missing where they should be present? The following strategies will help you understand your current culture:

- **Observe social interactions.** Social interactions will help you understand the health of the relational environment in your organization. Do people seek each other out or avoid contact? How much do people seem to enjoy each other's company? How do people interact? Do they connect on breaks? How do staff and management engage with each other?
- **Observe emotions**. The emotional climate of an organization is

an important indicator of the prevailing culture. Are people laughing? Are they excited about the organization's successes? Do people look up and smile when you walk past their workspaces? In times of frustration or conflict, do people respond constructively?

- **Assess the physical environment.** Is your workspace welcoming and interesting, or is it cold and boring? Look for personalization in individual work areas – are there family photos, plants, and various knickknacks that make the spaces feel homey and inviting? How is work space allocated, and why is it set up that way? Where are people located and why? How do people's locations affect their ability to interact? What is displayed on boards and walls? Are there welcoming common spaces, and are they being used?

- **Talk to people.** Interview employees either individually or in small focus groups. When talking about culture in small groups, it can be just as helpful to observe behaviors and interactions as it is to listen to words. Encourage people to consider what they like about the organization's culture and what they would like to improve or change. Remember that discussing organizational culture can be abstract for people. These questions can help tease out information about culture:

  - "How would you respond if a friend asked you, 'What's it like to work in your organization?'"
  - "What are the best things about the way we do our work?"
  - "How would you describe the relational atmosphere of our organization?"
  - "What is the main thing you'd like to see changed or improved in our organization?"

- **Use an assessment tool.** It can often be helpful to use a survey or some other tool to assess your culture. Either use an existing survey (for an example, see the Cultural Health Assessment tool, on page 216 in the Resources section) or create your own questions after you've done some initial work to understand your organization's culture. You can tailor the survey to gather more detailed information about aspects of the culture you've already observed.

- **Consider asking for external help.** Given the difficulty of seeing culture clearly from within, organizations often find it valuable to work with an outside consultant who can see things impartially from a fresh perspective. We recently worked with an organization that described itself as warm and welcoming. When we got there, we were greeted by a lengthy and very wide hallway with no paintings or furniture – just sterile white walls. Warm and welcoming were the furthest words from our minds as we walked down the hall!

As you work to understand culture, remember that many factors that influence culture cannot necessarily be observed in relationships or behaviors. While this is not an exhaustive list, remember to consider additional factors such as these:

- Leadership
- Internal structures
- Decision making processes
- Incentives
- Communication patterns
- Human resources policies
- Physical structures

Your focus should be broad enough to encompass all of these areas. Work to understand how each area affects individual and group behaviors.

As your culture change team begins their work, they must remember that some aspects of the existing culture are valuable and should be kept. Though identifying problem areas is often easier, be sure to look for the strengths of your current culture and consider the ways in which people are already functioning well. It's also important to keep in mind that there may be aspects of your culture that only need to be modified slightly in order to bring about desired behaviors.

It can be helpful to systematically list the "keeps" and the "discards" in simple descriptive language. By naming what is good about your existing culture, you can anchor desired changes in your current strengths. Just as individuals do better when they build on their strengths, so do teams and organizations.

When thinking about problem areas, the culture change team should begin by identifying the themes that keep coming up. What causes the greatest amount of frustration among staff? Pay attention to the stories that people share repeatedly. Recurring stories reveal how people make sense of their culture, and they can often illustrate both problem areas and strengths.

After your team has identified the aspects of your culture that should be kept and those that need to be changed, two steps are necessary: First, continue to validate and reinforce the desirable parts of your culture. Highlight those areas that are consistent with your culture change vision. Second, decide how to change the parts you don't like. As you do this, remember to *make small and easy changes now* by isolating the cultural elements that can be quickly reinforced or quickly eliminated.

PHASE 2: ENVISION A DESIRED CULTURE

One of the best ways to envision a new culture is to look at other organizational cultures for examples of what yours might become. Visit other organizations that you admire. Interview people from outside your workplace and ask them what they like about where they work.

In addition, your culture change team should share the results of Phase 1 with the individuals and groups they initially consulted and ask them to continue to envision a brighter future. Share your culture change team's vision throughout the organization and listen to how staff respond. Ask them what they would add or adjust in the vision and take their comments seriously. Not only does this show that you care about creating a healthy workplace culture, it also demonstrates that you value everyone's opinion.

The danger of failing to include everyone within the organization during this phase is that your vision for a new culture will lack buy-in from the people you need it from the most. Throughout the whole process of culture change, you must walk alongside all members of your organization, not just a select few.

Your senior leaders and culture change team must then engage in *focused planning* based on what they have learned. As you do this, make sure to consider the six main elements of healthy workplace culture we discussed in previous chapters. Consider which of these areas need attention as you move toward the culture you desire:

- **Communicate your purpose and values.** How can you ensure that everyone within your organization understands its purpose and values? Once you've identified what your values and beliefs are, focus on helping employees connect their own work to the organization's greater purpose.
- **Provide meaningful work.** How much attention has the organization given to making sure that everyone has meaningful work? Focus on finding each person's true talents and giving them work that builds on their talents and provides them with satisfaction.
- **Focus your leadership team on people.** Are your leaders sufficiently aware of how they impact others in the workplace? Focus on teaching your leaders to care about staff as people, supporting them in their work while providing healthy levels of accountability.
- **Build meaningful relationships.** How strong are the relationships within your organization? Focus on building an environment in which relationships can grow and people can connect with each other across teams.
- **Create peak performing teams.** How well do people work together in team environments? Focus on helping staff collaborate, building diversity into your teams and capitalizing on collective intelligence.

- **Practice constructive conflict management.** How skilled are your employees and managers when it comes to working through conflict? Focus on training people to resolve differences quickly and directly.

The culture change team must then finalize and record a desired vision for the organization's culture. Remember that long, convoluted reports overwhelm readers and are not likely to be retained. Put in the hard work necessary to keep this document succinct so that it is easy to understand and remember. Ensure your vision is clear enough that everyone can imagine the culture change.

In your culture change document, be specific about *what* is actually changing. For example, statements like "become more client centered" are not helpful or inspiring. Instead, use descriptive language such as, "We will respond to every client complaint on social media with words of apology and thanks."

As you reach the end of the visioning process, it will become clear that some of your desired changes will not come quickly or easily but will require long-term attention and energy. As you follow the process outlined in this chapter, your team will need to develop careful strategies to address existing complex issues and implement new elements of culture. Be clear about the specific plan and set of procedures required to move from where you are today to your desired future.

PHASE 3: SHARE & TEACH THE CULTURE

Present your culture change document to everyone in the organization. Be clear that this is *your organization's* document. It is based on the input of all employees, and senior leadership has made a commitment to stand by it.

There are many different ways this information can be rolled out. A memo from the CEO's desk is *never* a sufficient way of communicating important information. You can have departmental meetings, an organization-wide town hall, or both. Be sure to make this *the* agenda.

Don't water down the culture change message by burying it among other priorities. This is important! *Culture* is the reason you are meeting.

No matter how you decide to share this information, you should be sure to answer these five questions with clarity and thoughtfulness:

- Why are you making the changes?
- How are the changes being made?
- When are you making the changes?
- Who is responsible for making the changes?
- How will you know when the culture has successfully changed?

As a result of discussing these questions, each person should be able to clearly understand their own role in the culture change process.

During the initial assessment phase, you likely identified problem areas that needed attention or skills that were missing among staff or managers. These can often be addressed by offering training. For example, if the workplace culture has always tolerated a high level of disrespectful behavior, a workshop about being respectful in the workplace is a great way to begin changing behaviors. Everyone within the organization should know not only what's expected of them, but also *how* to actually do what's expected of them.

Working With Problem Behavior

One of the biggest challenges in culture change is working with employees who are out of step with the organization's vision. In our experience, it is critical that problem behaviors are addressed as soon as possible. Here's a quick summary of our approach:

1. Discuss your observations with the employee. Note the organization's values and desired behaviors, and describe what you

observe in the employee's behavior. Do this without judgment – simply point out the difference and ask about it. Your job is to understand why they are using an approach that isn't congruent with the envisioned culture.

2. Consider the possibility that the employee may have been in step with the culture as it was, but they are not in step with the culture as it is currently being envisioned. If this is the case, acknowledge that their behavior worked in the past but will not work in the future.

3. Support the employee in working toward desired behaviors through coaching and regular check-ins. Continue to focus on which behaviors are congruent or incongruent.

4. If the employee does not want to make changes, support their departure from the organization. In some cases, employees voluntarily leave when they feel out of step with the culture. In other cases, you may have to ask people to leave. In either case, remember that the employee is not necessarily a "bad" person. Rather, there is a difference between their preferences and the organization's needs.

PHASE 4: MONITOR & PROVIDE ACCOUNTABILITY

Change will not occur or be sustained if you allow room for exceptions. Articulating a new way of doing things without holding people accountable will only create cynicism. If you are working to increase active participation in meetings, but you turn a blind eye when "Bill from accounting" refuses to put his phone away, you communicate that you aren't serious about culture change.

Instead, you must raise the matter with Bill and discuss the incongruity between his actions and the new expectations. Until you are willing to provide accountability and make the difficult decisions required to create, protect, and sustain a healthy culture, there will be no culture change. Rather, employees will snicker and roll their eyes at the "new" culture, which everyone knows will never come to be.

In addition to holding people accountable, you must also monitor the new processes that you have put in place. Remember that the phases of culture change act as a cycle. You will need to periodically check in and assess your culture's health. Use the strategies you employed in earlier phases: Walk around and observe how things have changed as a result of your organization's work so far. What do you notice about interactions and the environment? Check in with individuals and reconvene focus groups. Monitoring progress is crucial especially in the early stages of change because it is easy to revert to old behaviors.

To make change permanent, we have to recognize that our efforts must continue over time. People easily revert to the way things were because they already know how to function in the previous cultural environment without using as much energy. Habits are hard to change.

When I, Eric, was a teenager, I had never managed to floss for more than a day or two in a row even though my dentist told me I needed to change my habits if I wanted my teeth to last a lifetime. When I was just out of university, I read an article that said a new habit had to be practiced for 42 consecutive days in order to become routine. I wanted to test this theory out, so I decided to floss for 42 days straight. I brought my partner in on my plan, and she agreed to do it with me. This provided a level of accountability and social motivation that allowed my flossing experiment to succeed. I formed the habit, and now if I don't floss, I feel like something is missing from my day. This routine has now lasted for more than 20 years – or about 7,300 days!

In the same way, changing a workplace culture requires us to build new habits with other people and then practice those new ways of operating within relationships of accountability until they become our normal and natural ways of functioning. In an article titled "Leading Change: Why Transformation Efforts Fail," John P. Kotter writes: "Change sticks when it becomes 'the way we do things around here', when it seeps into the bloodstream of the corporate body. Until new behaviors are rooted in social norms and shared values, they are subject to degradation."[3]

When it comes to culture change, there will inevitably be bumps along the way. It is therefore important that you evaluate your progress throughout the culture change process. Evaluation, or checking in, also provides a measure of accountability, which helps sustain change.

Before you even begin your culture change process, determine *who* will evaluate your progress as well as *when* and *how* they will do it. Discuss what indicators will let you know whether you are moving in the right direction. Develop a clear idea of the changes you'll see when you've met your goals.

Evaluate whether your successes have met your original hopes for change. And be willing to adjust your goal if you realize that it was not ambitions enough or if it pointed you in the wrong direction.

A Manager Who No Longer Fits

In our consulting work, we once helped a CEO work through a major dilemma. After her organization went through a long-term culture change process, a member of her maintenance staff was confident enough to approach her and say, "I really like all that you're doing, but I've got to tell you, one of your senior managers isn't living this new culture."

The CEO took a long, hard look at the impact of this manager's behavior, asked some pointed questions to others in the organization, and came to the realization that this observation was true. The manager had not bought into the new culture, and he was in fact working to sabotage it. The CEO was torn about what to do. This manager had been a very valuable member of her team for a long time, and she appreciated his skill set. She knew it would be very difficult to replace him if she were to let him go.

After spending several months attempting to bring the manager on board, the CEO made the difficult decision to let him go. The organization lost knowledge and skills as a result, but ultimately, the CEO felt it was the best way to protect the new company culture.

COMMUNICATE, COMMUNICATE, COMMUNICATE

Throughout the entire culture change process, it is imperative that you communicate what is happening! Risk *over*-communicating rather than *under*-communicating. A common theme in our survey responses was a lack of communication from leaders. One participant wrote about the impact of poor communication: "Management could do a better job of communicating with other levels. When change occurs now, the rationale behind it is not articulated. As a result, not everyone can gain an understanding of the need for change." Another participant reported that the lack of communication "causes rumors and worry. People like to know what's going on, even if it's not good news – any news is better than no news."

Over the years, we have heard many excuses for insufficient communication from leadership, including these common ones:

- "Employees don't need to know yet. When the time comes we will tell them."
- "We've passed this over to human resources, and they will spread the news."
- "Everyone already knows – I attached a memo in my most recent email."

If a culture change team ever wonders whether they have communicated enough, they almost certainly have not. Because they are leading the process, the team is always a step or two ahead of everyone else in the organization – they are meeting regularly, reviewing information, and discussing the issues. It is easy for them to assume that others throughout the organization are in a similar place to them in terms of their processing and need for information. This simply isn't so. The most important solution to this problem is regular communication.

Drawing on William Bridges' book, *Managing Transitions*,[4] we recommend that culture change leaders focus on these four areas in their communication with the rest of the organization:

- **The reasons behind the need for culture change**. Some people will need to be reminded that there was a problem with the culture that needed to change. If they had not experienced the old culture as problematic, they might find it difficult to leave behind old ways, particularly when the new ways aren't yet fully realized. Make sure staff remember that there was an impetus for change.
- **The process for change.** In the transition from the old to the new, employees will need to be confident in the culture change process. Demonstrate that there is a plan for making the envisioned culture a reality. When people can't see the way forward, it's often easier to return to what was familiar.
- **The roles people will play in the change.** At a concrete level, each person will need to know what part they will play in making the new vision a reality. Staff will need to be confident about what they should and should not do. When they are aware of their roles, they will be more focused on the practical ways they can contribute to the new culture.
- **The vision for a better culture.** Everyone needs to keep the vision for the new culture in mind. Communicating the vision keeps people oriented in the right direction. The vision should be compelling enough that it provides motivation for the hard work of getting there.

As you work at changing your culture, focusing on each of these areas in your communication enables staff to participate in the journey of culture transformation. In their book *Change the Culture, Change the Game*, Roger Connors and Tom Smith note that culture change will only be successful "when everyone's actions, beliefs, and experiences are aligned from person to person and across the various functions of the company."[5] Communication is the key to reaching this alignment.

Influencing Culture as an Employee

For employees who care about culture, it can be frustrating to see the need for change but not have the authority to make things happen. However, it is important to remember that, regardless of our role within an organization, we all play an important part in creating a healthy workplace culture. By communicating effectively and supporting the people we work with, we can influence change. If you are an employee, here are two ways you can support the process of building a healthier workplace culture:

Raise Concerns About Culture With Your Manager

Find a time when you can have your manager's full attention. Managers are often caught up in the busyness of day-to-day demands, and they may not be aware of the issues you observe.

- Be clear about the issue. Describe the problem and explain how it impacts employees, productivity, or quality of work.
- Ground your observations in the interest of both your manager *and* the organization as a whole. Acknowledge both the strengths and the weaknesses of your workplace, and explain why the issue should matter to everyone.
- Offer solutions. Don't just name the problem — suggest ways of improving the situation as well. Consider the ways in which a change in culture could help the organization accomplish its mission more effectively.

Look for Workplace Allies

It may be helpful to look for coworkers who are also interested in your organization's health and culture. Coworkers often share obstacles and concerns that are best addressed collaboratively.

- Ask about your coworker's perspective and whether they have noticed the issues you've identified. You may be able to clarify why things are the way they are, or they may agree that a change is needed and work with you to make change.
- As you discuss your workplace culture, be careful not to focus only on problems and complaints. Speak as well about what you believe is possible, and explain your positive goals for the workplace.
- Approach leadership with your ideas and concerns – sooner rather than later – in the manner described above.

While management may not always respond to your concerns in the way you would like, they will likely appreciate your efforts if you communicate your intent to help the organization. Though not everyone has the power to take control of an organization's culture, every person can influence culture change by focusing their efforts on what matters to the organization, communicating clearly, and inviting others to collaborate.

SUSTAINING CHANGE

Every spring, I, Randy, plant a vegetable garden. For a while, I tend to it daily. I water the plants, and I keep the weeds away by carefully tilling the soil and mulching. About a month into the growing season, my garden usually looks like an image from *Better Homes and Gardens* magazine. And then I go on vacation for a few weeks. When I return, the garden is overrun with weeds. Some plants are doing well, but others are not.

If your organization has always been healthy, or if you have worked hard to develop a workplace culture that you are proud of, the next challenge is sustaining that culture. Organizational culture is like a garden: without attention, it will not thrive. Weeds will come in and overtake the once idyllic green space.

Sustaining change requires ongoing attention to the six key elements of healthy workplace culture that we have described in the previous chapters. Just as effective leaders don't ever feel that they have arrived, healthy organizations do not become complacent either. Instead, they continually revisit and reinforce those things that make their workplace culture healthy. Just like gardeners, effective leaders need to ask themselves what needs fertilizer and what needs to be weeded in order to maintain organizational health.

As you discern what needs to be reinforced and what should be rooted out, your culture change document can provide an anchor for maintaining your newly identified values, target behaviors, and processes. Sustaining healthy culture requires us to assess and monitor our culture, making changes and adaptations along the way. Culture change is a journey that never actually ends.

CHANGE TAKES TIME

While it's tempting to try to fix everything right away, the reality is that culture change takes time. Pace yourself. Set short-term goals that lead you along the path toward your long-term goals. Gather your team, discuss specific, tangible changes you want to see, and then make a plan with a timetable for implementation. Instead of working toward ten different objectives at the same time, begin by focusing on two or three. These short-term goals will build upon each other and form the basis for longer-term change.

We have met many people who have had great intentions for changing their organization's culture. They attend a workshop, read a book, or go on a retreat and become inspired by what their organization could become. Then they wake up and go to work to find that the daily grind and rhythm of their tasks get in the way of working on culture.

Organizational culture change requires more than a desire for a better future. Changing culture is not an event but a process – and a long process at that. A commitment to changing culture means a serious investment of time and energy. It must be seen as essential work that involves everyone, including senior leadership. With a clear plan, change is possible.

QUESTIONS FOR REFLECTION

1. Are there any signs that it's time to change your culture? What are they?
2. If culture change is needed, who are the key people who could lead this change?
3. What small and simple changes to your culture could you make today?
4. If you already have a healthy culture, what do you need to continue to reinforce? What do you need to be vigilant about preventing?

Conclusion

FRIDAY NIGHT CONVERSATIONS

It's Friday night. For many, the work week is done. You decide to go to a restaurant for a nice evening meal, and the hostess sits you close to a group of friends – so close that you can't help but overhear their conversation as they go around the table, each talking in turn about their weeks at work.

One utters, "Thank God it's Friday. I hate my job." Another belts out, "My manager is such a jerk – he doesn't listen to anyone." And another chimes in, "I have no idea why what we do even matters. Every day I feel like I'm stuck in a prison." On and on it goes until the final person at the table clears her throat to speak.

As she begins, you recognize the voice and suddenly realize: she is *your* employee. What is she about to say? Will she continue in the same vein as her friends? Or will she instead say something like: "I feel for all of you. I actually like where I work. I feel connected to what we're doing and the people I work with. It's a great place to work"?

As leaders, we need to consider what is said during these Friday night, end-of-week conversations among friends and loved ones. Are people proud of your work culture? Is your organization a place where people like to work? Or is it one that people disparage? The answers to these questions should be instructive and motivate us to pay attention to our work cultures.

TWO QUESTIONS

As we wrote in the introduction to this book, "the culture question" has two parts: "How does your organization's culture impact how much people like where they work?" and "What can you do to make it better?" In this book, we have shown that culture does indeed impact whether or not people like where they work. We have also shown how leaders can improve culture and create healthier workplaces where people like to work.

The chapters in this book do not offer a step-by-step process. Rather, they provide guidance regarding the elements that we believe are central to all great workplace cultures. Essentially, this book provides a map, but each of us decides the route we will take for the journey.

Maps help us plan, and they guide us along our travels. However, maps do not always show us all the obstacles and opportunities we may encounter along the way – there may be a scenic side road that doesn't look like much on the map or a restaurant with great food that just opened up. We need to be flexible with our routes and willing to stop, change direction, or enjoy the scenery. But we still need a map. Otherwise we cannot plan where we are going, and we risk getting lost.

This book is primarily a map of the journey that we, the authors, have traveled. We hope you proceed from here with the map we've provided. Don't just put the book down and think of workplace culture as something you will eventually get to. You are already contributing to workplace culture, and this book is an invitation to be more intentional. Talk about it with others in your organization. Ask the question, "What are our employees saying on Friday nights?" Develop a plan to begin the journey of creating, improving, and sustaining a healthy workplace culture.

THE JOURNEY FORWARD

One of the most meaningful things we can do with our time is to help to create workplaces where people like to work. But it's not only about our well-being – it's also about the sustainability of our organizations. Healthy cultures are durable cultures. No matter what industry you are in, having a healthy workplace culture is truly one of the best competitive advantages. Other organizations may have access to more funding, or they may have greater capabilities in certain domains, but if they do not have healthy cultures, they will not be successful in the long run.

At ACHIEVE, we have days, weeks, and even extended periods of time when things aren't as great as they should be. But overall, we have a healthy culture – one that we have developed over time. And we trust that, with attention, it will stand the test of time. We are confident that on Friday nights, our employees are the alternative voices to many in the crowd – voices that tell their peers and loved ones that they like where they work.

This is what we wish for you and for everyone in the workforce. Our hope for this book is that it will assist you on your culture journey as you work to transform your organization into a place where people like to work.

Survey Analysis

Throughout this book, we have highlighted results from our Culture Question Survey. We conducted this survey as part of our research to gain insight into which factors contribute to, or are connected to, having a great workplace. In the survey, we asked both managers and employees to rate 20 statements on a five-point scale, choosing between Strongly Disagree, Disagree, Neutral, Agree, and Strongly Agree. Here is the full list of statements included in the survey:

1. My organization is a great place to work.
2. Leaders in my organization communicate the organization's purpose in meaningful ways.
3. I like the people I work with.
4. Leaders in my organization care about healthy interactions between employees.
5. The work I do challenges me in a positive way.
6. My organization produces high-quality work.
7. I can rely on my coworkers.
8. My direct supervisor cares about me as a person.
9. My organization has a meaningful purpose.
10. I have a friend at work.
11. Leaders in my organization work to resolve conflict quickly.
12. The work I do brings me personal satisfaction.
13. I am motivated and engaged at work.
14. Teamwork is a source of positive energy at my place of work.
15. I trust my direct supervisor.
16. I have fun at work.

17. People in my workplace deal with conflict constructively.

18. I am challenged and inspired by others at work.

19. Leaders in my organization communicate effectively.

20. I have autonomy in how I do my work.

We collected responses by displaying the survey on our website, linking to it on social media platforms, and emailing it to our current clients and contacts.

We did not use a randomized sampling method, so our results cannot be generalized to the broader population within a certain margin of error. We believe that our results are *practically* significant even though they are not statistically significant. This means that we believe the results of our survey are applicable for decision making, and we have found that it has produced valuable information and insights into the factors that relate to having a great workplace. The results have clearly shown which variables are most impactful for creating a workplace where people like to work. While we cannot be certain that our results accurately reflect the opinions of the general population, we can say that they reflect the diverse opinions of 2,401 managers and employees of various ages, working in both small and large organizations across many different sectors.

One of the guiding beliefs of ACHIEVE Centre for Leadership & Workplace Performance is that people should be able to like where they work, and we provide training and resources to this end. Therefore, in sending this survey to existing clients and those who follow us on social media – that is, people who may already be interested in workplace improvement – we assume that a greater proportion of respondents identified as having a great workplace than if we had selected participants at random. The practical significance of our survey lies in the relationships between having a great place to work and the other factors we asked about related to workplace culture. The important questions to ask are: "What factors are connected to having a great workplace?" and "How do those factors contribute to having a great workplace or not?"

For the purposes of this analysis, people who "have a great workplace" are those who responded with Agree or Strongly Agree to, "My organization is a great place to work." Likewise, those who "do not have a great workplace" are those who responded Disagree or Strongly Disagree to this statement.

We used correlation as a tool to analyze our data. Correlation measures the strength of relationships between variables – in this case, our survey statements. For example, we wanted to analyze the relationship between having a great place to work and reporting that you are cared for as a person by a direct supervisor. Correlation is measured by the correlation coefficient, which is abbreviated in this analysis as "r." It can range from -1 to 1, and the closer it is to -1 or 1, the stronger the two variables are negatively or positively related. A coefficient of 0 means that there is no relation between the variables. When looking at positive relationships, a coefficient of 0.2 to 0.3 is weak, 0.31 to 0.5 moderate, and 0.51 to 1.0 is strong. A strong positive relationship means that as one variable increases, the other increases. Correlation should be used as a general guideline for establishing relationship strengths between variables, but does not show causation, or which variable causes the other.

This analysis focuses on 10 of the statements in which we found strong or interesting connections to having a great workplace, including weak correlations where we thought we would find strong correlations. When numbers do not add up to 100%, this is due to rounding to the nearest whole number. We explore these in the order that they appeared in the survey.

My organization is a great place to work.
A strong majority of our respondents reported that their organization is a great place to work. While 77% of respondents agreed or strongly agreed, only 15% were neutral, and 9% disagreed or strongly disagreed. As stated above, it is likely that this result was skewed due to our sampling method, so we have not directly referenced this result in the chapters. However, we believe that it is significant to look at the relationships between having a great place to work and the other survey statements.

Leaders in my organization communicate the organization's purpose in meaningful ways.

Our survey data showed that having leaders who communicate their organization's purpose in meaningful ways has a strong positive relationship with having a great workplace (r=0.69). This means that workplaces in which leaders communicate meaningfully about the organization's purpose are more likely to be great workplaces.

In addition to the strong correlation, this relationship seems quite intuitive. Both statements in our survey that are about communication have a strong relationship with having a great workplace (see "Leaders in my organization communicate effectively" on page 199 below). The statement, "Leaders in my organization communicate the organization's purpose in meaningful ways" specifically connects effective communication with a sense of purpose, both of which have an impact on workplace health. When leaders both communicate effectively and convey a sense of meaning and purpose, workers are more likely to appreciate and enjoy their work experience.

Of respondents who agreed or strongly agreed that they have a great workplace, 75% agreed or strongly agreed that leaders in their organization communicate the organization's purpose in meaningful ways. Only 7% disagreed or strongly disagreed. The reverse trend holds true for those who do not have a great workplace. Of those respondents, 78% disagreed or strongly disagreed that leaders in their organization communicate the organization's purpose in meaningful ways, and only 9% agreed.

"Leaders in my organization communicate the organization's purpose in meaningful ways," of those who agree or strongly agree that they have a great workplace.

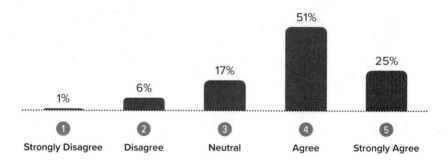

"Leaders in my organization communicate the organization's purpose in meaningful ways," of those who disagree or strongly disagree that they have a great workplace.

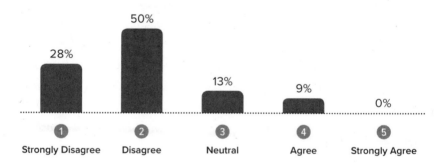

Leaders in my organization care about healthy interactions between employees.

Our survey data showed that having leaders who care about healthy employee interactions and having a great workplace have a strong positive relationship (r=0.68). The fact that workplace satisfaction increases when healthy interactions are encouraged gives a strong indication that the promotion of healthy relationships is one of the contributing factors to having a great workplace.

This strong correlation makes logical sense. When leadership is involved in creating and participating in a culture of healthy interactions, employees build positive relationships with each other and with leaders, resulting in a sense of well-being in the workplace.

Of respondents who agreed or strongly agreed that they have a great workplace, 79% agreed or strongly agreed that leaders in their organization care about healthy interactions between employees. Only 6% disagreed or strongly disagreed. The reverse trend persists for those who do not have a great workplace. Of those respondents, 73% disagreed or strongly disagreed that leaders in their organization care about healthy interactions between employees, and only 8% agreed or strongly agreed.

For most of the other statements, the differences between the responses of managers and employees were minimal. However, for, "Leaders in my organization care about healthy interactions between employees," the differences were much more apparent. This could be indicative of the differences in how people perceive the intentions of leadership. Of the respondents who do not have a great workplace, 77% of managers and 68% of employees disagreed or strongly disagreed that leaders in their organization care about healthy interactions between employees. More significantly, of those who do not have a great workplace, 41% of managers and 26% of employees strongly disagreed. This could indicate that those with management responsibilities have a more critical view of leadership or that they are more directly affected by senior leadership.

"Leaders in my organization care about healthy interactions between employees," of those who agree or strongly agree that they have a great workplace.

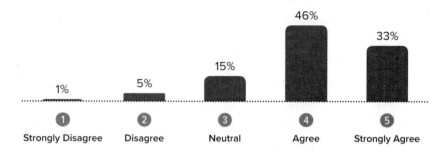

"Leaders in my organization care about healthy interactions between employees," of those who disagree or strongly disagree that they have a great workplace.

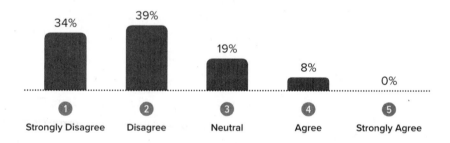

My organization produces high-quality work.

Our data showed a strong positive relationship between working for an organization that produces high-quality work and having a great workplace (r=0.65). This means that the people who strongly agreed that their organization produces high-quality work were more likely to strongly agree that they have a great workplace.

Of respondents who have a great workplace, a very strong majority (91%) agreed or strongly agreed that their workplace produces high-quality work. Almost no one (1%) disagreed or strongly disagreed. On the other end, of respondents who do not have a great workplace, the distribution was more even. While 40% disagreed or strongly disagreed that their workplace produces high-quality work, 27% agreed or strongly agreed, and 33% were neutral.

There are at least two possible reasons for this. It's possible that people who are happy at work tend to think highly of their work, with the inverse also being true. Or it could mean that when work is high quality, people take pride in it, leading them to think more highly of their workplace.

There is a noticeable difference between managers and employees in workplaces that are not great. In those workplaces, 17% of employees agree or strongly agree that their workplace produces high-quality work, but 35% of managers agree or strongly agree. This suggests that managers who do not think they have a great workplace may have a different impression of the quality of their organization's work because of their position. It also suggests that, for these managers, producing high-quality work has less of a connection to whether they think their workplace is a great place to work. We surmise that because managers have more control over the work, they are more likely to judge it positively.

"My organization produces high-quality work," of those who agree or strongly agree that they have a great workplace.

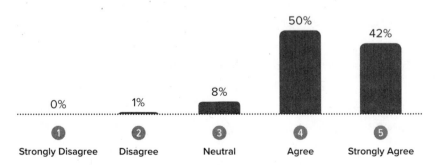

"My organization produces high-quality work," of those who disagree or strongly disagree that they have a great workplace.

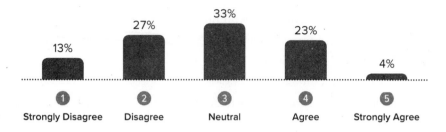

"My organization produces high-quality work," of those who disagree or strongly disagree that they have a great workplace.

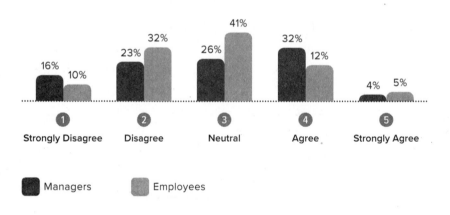

My direct supervisor cares about me as a person.

Our survey data showed that there is a positive relationship between having a great workplace and having a caring supervisor (r=0.54). This means that workplaces where leaders care about employees are more likely to be great workplaces. The fact that satisfaction with one's workplace increases when leaders are caring indicates that caring leadership is one of the contributing factors to having a great workplace. It is noteworthy that, of any two statements in our survey, "My direct supervisor cares about me as a person" and "I trust my direct supervisor" have the strongest relationship (r=0.84). We infer that people are more willing to trust someone if they feel like that person cares about them. Interestingly, neither of these statements has an exceptionally strong relationship with any other statement.

This statement is not as strongly related to having a great workplace as some of the other statements. This indicates that while caring leadership is a factor in creating positive workplaces, it must be coupled with other leadership and workplace culture factors. It is not enough for a leader to care about people without being effective in other areas.

It is common for great workplaces to have leaders who care about employees. Of respondents who agreed or strongly agreed that they have a great workplace, 82% agreed or strongly agreed that their supervisor cares about them as a person, and only 5% disagreed or strongly disagreed. Caring leadership is less common, but it is not wholly absent in workplaces that are not great. Of those who disagreed or strongly disagreed that they have a great workplace, 53% disagreed or strongly disagreed that their supervisor cares about them as a person, and 31% agreed or strongly agreed that their leader cares about them.

"My direct supervisor cares about me as a person," of those who agree or strongly agree that they have a great workplace.

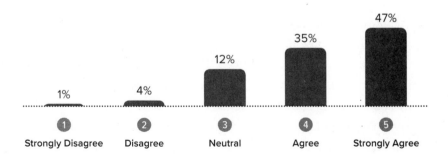

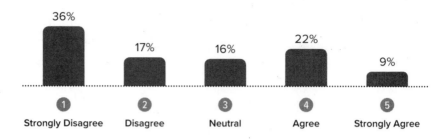

"My direct supervisor cares about me as a person," of those who disagree or strongly disagree that they have a great workplace.

36%	17%	16%	22%	9%
①	②	③	④	⑤
Strongly Disagree	Disagree	Neutral	Agree	Strongly Agree

My organization has a meaningful purpose.

Our data showed a positive relationship between working for an organization with a meaningful purpose and having a great workplace (r=0.55). This means people are more likely to believe that they have a great workplace when they also believe that their workplace has a meaningful purpose.

By comparison, the statement, "Leaders in my organization communicate the organization's purpose in meaningful ways" has a much stronger relationship with having a great workplace (r=0.69). This suggests that communicating about an organization's purpose in meaningful ways is more impactful than actually having a meaningful purpose. In fact, according to our data, having leaders who communicate organizational purpose in meaningful ways and working at an organization with a meaningful purpose only have a moderate relationship (r=0.48). This means that neither of these is a great indicator of the other. We believe this means that leaders are able to inspire workers by speaking meaningfully about their organization even if that organization does not necessarily have a meaningful purpose. The important distinction is that one of the statements is about meaningful communication and the other is about meaningful organizational purpose.

Of respondents who have a great workplace, virtually everyone

(98%) agreed or strongly agreed that their workplace has a meaningful purpose. Almost no one disagreed or strongly disagreed. On the other end, of respondents who do not have a great workplace, 22% disagreed or strongly disagreed that their workplace has a meaningful purpose, while 62% agreed or strongly agreed.

"My organization has a meaningful purpose," of those who agree or strongly agree that they have a great workplace.

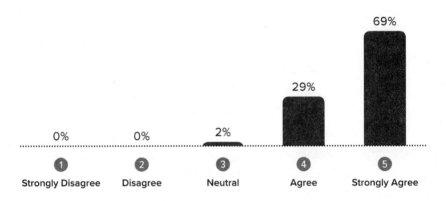

"My organization has a meaningful purpose," of those who disagree or strongly disagree that they have a great workplace.

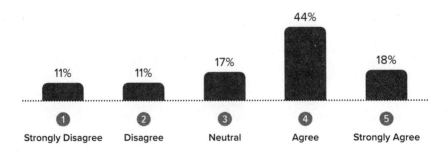

I have a friend at work.

The correlation between having a great workplace and having a friend at work is fairly weak (r=0.24), which suggests that there is not a significant link between them. Of all the statements in the survey, having a friend has the lowest correlation with having a great workplace by a significant margin. This does not mean that meaningful relationships are not significant in creating great workplaces. We believe meaningful relationships extend beyond friendships.

The responses to this statement indicate that having a friend at work is not a great indicator of whether or not an individual thinks they have a great workplace. In both great and not great workplaces, people will often find a friend with whom they can relate. Negative workplaces inherently act as a source of bonding – employees can confide in each other about how they really feel about their workplace.

For those who agreed that they have a great workplace, 79% of respondents agreed or strongly agreed that they have a friend at work, and only 6% disagreed or strongly disagreed.

Among those who disagreed that they have a great workplace, the results are more mixed. However, a majority (62%) of those who do not have a great workplace have a friend at work, and 20% of respondents disagreed or strongly disagreed that they have a friend at work.

"I have a friend at work," of those who agree or strongly agree that they have a great workplace.

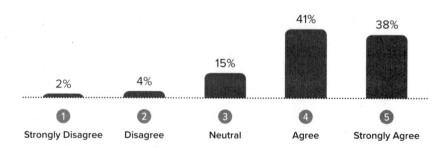

Strongly Disagree	Disagree	Neutral	Agree	Strongly Agree
2%	4%	15%	41%	38%

"I have a friend at work," of those who disagree or strongly disagree that they have a great workplace.

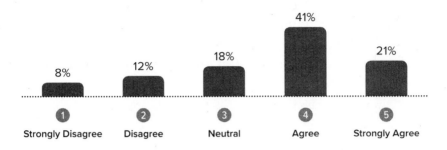

8%   12%   18%   41%   21%

1 — Strongly Disagree   2 — Disagree   3 — Neutral   4 — Agree   5 — Strongly Agree

Leaders in my organization work to resolve conflict quickly.

Our data showed that having leaders who resolve conflict quickly has a strong relationship with having a great workplace (r=0.61). By comparison, the statement, "People in my workplace deal with conflict constructively" had a noticeably weaker correlation with having a great workplace (r=0.54). This indicates that leaders have a more substantial role than employees when it comes to conflict resolution and its relationship to creating a great workplace. Interestingly, "People in my workplace deal with conflict constructively" and "Leaders in my organization work to resolve conflict quickly" had one of the strongest correlations in our survey results (r=0.70). This emphasizes that when it comes to conflict, leaders should lead by example. In workplaces where leaders resolve conflict quickly, others are far more likely to resolve conflict constructively as well.

Respondents were more neutral to this statement than some of the other statements. Of those who reported having a great workplace, 61% agreed or strongly agreed that leaders in their organization resolve conflict quickly, 26% were neutral, and 13% disagreed or strongly disagreed.

The response was stronger for those who did not agree that they have a great workplace. A large majority (82%) disagreed or strongly disagreed that leaders in their organization resolve conflict quickly, 11% were neutral, and 7% agreed or strongly agreed. This shows that workplaces that are *not* great are more likely to lack leadership that works to resolve conflict quickly than great workplaces are to have leaders who are noticed for working to resolve conflict quickly.

It may seem surprising that more people in great workplaces chose "Neutral" as a response to whether their leaders deal with conflict quickly. One explanation could be that great workplaces have a lower incidence of negative conflict in general, and when there is conflict, it is dealt with privately and quickly. If conflict is not regularly apparent, it is difficult for constructive conflict resolution to be apparent as well. However, in a workplace where conflict is more commonly perceived, it is easy to see when conflict is dealt with and when it is not. People notice conflict most when it is not handled well. In environments where it is handled very well, it may not be noticed at all.

"Leaders in my organization work to resolve conflict quickly," of those who agree or strongly agree that they have a great workplace.

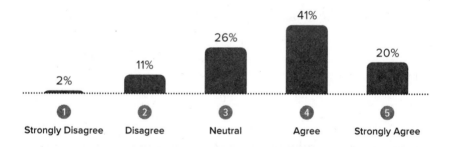

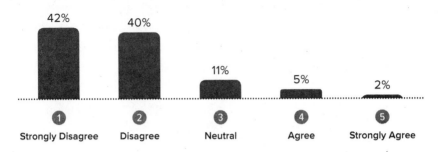

"Leaders in my organization work to resolve conflict quickly," of those who disagree or strongly disagree that they have a great workplace.

42%	40%	11%	5%	2%
1	2	3	4	5
Strongly Disagree	Disagree	Neutral	Agree	Strongly Agree

The work I do brings me personal satisfaction.

Our data showed that doing work that brings personal satisfaction has a moderate positive relationship with having a great workplace ($r=0.48$). This suggests that having work that brings personal satisfaction is a less significant factor in connection with having a great workplace.

The correlation is only moderate likely because many people find personal satisfaction in their work even if they do not have a great workplace. Of those who reported having a great workplace, 93% agreed or strongly agreed that their work brings them personal satisfaction. Only 1% disagreed or strongly disagreed.

Just over half (52%) of those who do not have a great workplace reported that their work brings them personal satisfaction. For a quarter (26%), their work does not. A similar portion (22%) is neutral about their work bringing them personal satisfaction.

It is interesting that finding personal satisfaction does not have a strong connection to having a great workplace. Of all our survey statements, this has the second weakest correlation with having a great workplace, stronger only than, "I have a friend at work." It seems that people can find personal satisfaction regardless of whether they have a great workplace. Personal satisfaction is clearly more common in great workplaces, but the majority of our survey respondents who do not have a great workplace still find personal satisfaction in their work.

Just as people can find friends at work even if they do not have a great workplace, they can also find satisfaction in their work. This statement has to do with a personal connection to specific work, so workers may be able to direct their work in a way that brings them satisfaction even in a workplace that they do not think is great.

"The work I do brings me personal satisfaction," of those who agree or strongly agree that they have a great workplace.

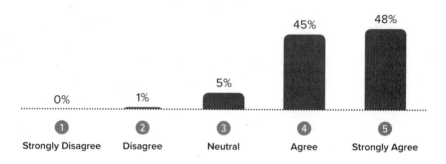

"The work I do brings me personal satisfaction," of those who disagree or strongly disagree that they have a great workplace.

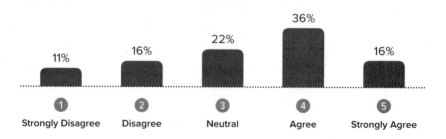

Leaders in my organization communicate effectively.

This statement has a strong relationship with having a great workplace (r=0.65). Effective communication from leadership contributes more to a great work environment than two of the five other statements related to leaders: "My direct supervisor cares about me as a person" (r=0.54) and "I trust my direct supervisor" (r=0.55). One explanation for this may be that the two latter statements relate to direct supervisors, but the first one relates to leaders in general. If leaders *at all levels* communicate effectively, this may have more of an impact on having a great workplace than one's *direct supervisor* being caring or trustworthy. All the statements that deal with leaders in general have higher correlations with having a great workplace than the two questions that relate only to direct supervisors.

Over half (60%) of respondents who have a great workplace also agreed or strongly agreed that their leaders communicate effectively, and 27% were neutral. However, the much larger majority (87%) of those who disagreed or strongly disagreed that they have a great workplace disagreed or strongly disagreed that their leaders communicate effectively.

One possible explanation for this is that people who believe that they have a great workplace do not notice the effect that communication has on their workplace. The benefit may be normalized in a workplace's culture, causing employees to not realize the difference it makes. In a negative workplace, it is much easier to see that effective communication is missing. Similar to effective conflict resolution, effective communication is noticed more in its absence than its presence.

"Leaders in my organization communicate effectively," of those who agree or strongly agree that they have a great workplace.

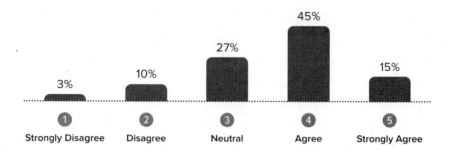

3%	10%	27%	45%	15%
①	②	③	④	⑤
Strongly Disagree	**Disagree**	**Neutral**	**Agree**	**Strongly Agree**

"Leaders in my organization communicate effectively," of those who disagree or strongly disagree that they have a great workplace.

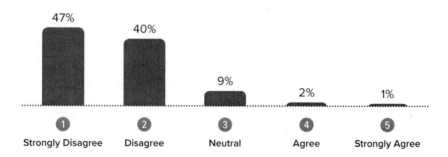

47%	40%	9%	2%	1%
①	②	③	④	⑤
Strongly Disagree	**Disagree**	**Neutral**	**Agree**	**Strongly Agree**

Conclusion

These findings show us where we should be focusing our efforts as we strive to create workplaces where people like to work. The data from our survey make two trends apparent to us.

First, of the five statements that have the strongest correlation with having a great workplace, four of them have to do with the conduct of leaders. Specifically, leaders have significant influence on the quality of a workplace by communicating the organization's purpose in meaningful ways, caring about healthy interactions between employees, communicating effectively, and working to resolve conflict quickly.

Second, some factors are more significant in their absence than in their presence. For example, when effective conflict resolution and communication are present in a workplace, it is not always easy to notice their impacts. However, the absence of these factors has a strong negative influence on a workplace, as shown in the correlation data of our survey. This means that leaders and employees must be mindful to practice effective communication and conflict resolution, even though their efforts may not be recognized.

Although our survey did not measure the personal efforts of non-leadership employees in creating great workplaces, we believe that the actions of all staff matter. As our research indicates, leaders bear a larger share of the responsibility for building the conditions for an organization to thrive, given their position of power. However, great workplaces are co-created by everyone. All organizations are the sum of their parts – the individual actions, attitudes, and efforts of each person.

Reading Recommendations

OUR TOP 10 BOOKS RELATED TO WORKPLACE CULTURE
While this list could easily be longer, these are the books that have inspired us most to think about organizational culture in new and different ways.

Delivering Happiness: A Path to Profits, Passion, and Purpose
by Tony Hsieh (Business Plus, 2010)

Tony Hsieh, CEO of Zappos, provides a compelling account of what it takes to build a unique and healthy organization. We appreciate Hsieh's focus on the relationship between his organization's corporate culture and the priority of making both customers *and* everyone else happy, including their suppliers. This book is particularly inspiring for those who are interested in building a great culture while also providing customer service at a very high level.

> *Culture became our number one priority, even more important than customer service. We thought that if we got the culture right, then building our brand to be about the very best customer service would happen naturally on its own.... To keep our culture strong, we wanted to make sure that we only hired people who we would also enjoy hanging out with outside the office. As it turned out, many of the best ideas came about while having drinks at a local bar* (page 134).

Drive: The Surprising Truth About What Motivates Us
by Daniel H. Pink (Riverhead Books, 2009)

This well-researched book challenges assumptions about motivation and provides a new lens through which to view employee engagement. Through compelling stories, Pink provides practical ways for leaders and organizations to increase motivation. We appreciate Pink's accessible writing style and really like that the book has been designed in a way that is easy to refer back to when needed.

The most successful people, the evidence shows, often aren't directly pursuing conventional notions of success. They're working hard and persisting through difficulties because of their internal desire to control their lives, learn about their world, and accomplish something that endures (page 77).

Flow: The Psychology of Optimal Experience
by Mihaly Csikszentmihalyi (Harper & Row, 1990)

Having been through 127 editions since it was first published in 1990, this book has stood the test of time and helps demonstrate the importance of meaningful work as a key to healthy workplace culture. Csikszentmihalyi provides a comprehensive analysis of "flow," or what is commonly referred to as "being in the zone." As he explains it, flow can be achieved when our ability matches the challenge of a task. One of his overarching premises is that being in a state of flow produces happiness. While this book is not specifically written with workplace culture in mind, its insights are still very applicable to personal and workplace contexts.

Because work is so universal, yet so varied, it makes a tremendous difference to one's overall contentment whether what one does for a living is enjoyable or not.... It is true that if one finds flow in work, and in relations to other people, one is well on the way toward improving the quality of life as a whole (page 144).

Harvard Business Review
(Harvard Business Publishing, est. 1922)

It's technically not a book, but we've found this magazine to be a treasure trove of research and real-life case studies. Each issue has a theme such as employee happiness or using purpose to drive performance. Many of its themes address issues that we believe to be the cornerstones of healthy workplace culture. A subscription gives readers online access to an extensive library of back issues, which means that when we're looking for well-researched and fresh information on any management topic, the *HBR* database is the place to start. To get started, be sure to check out the articles that we reference in this book on pages 219–22.

Joy, Inc.: How We Built a Workplace People Love
by Richard Sheridan (Penguin Group, 2015)

We like books that use real examples to share ideas and insights. This book is full of stories that demonstrate the importance of putting employee happiness first. Using examples of approaches that have worked, and others that have failed, Sheridan presents meaningful ideas for creating workplaces that are more joyful. We also appreciate that Sheridan is "working in the trenches" as the CEO, not writing about workplace culture from the outside looking in.

Easy change is neither lasting nor meaningful. If you choose joy, know that you are at the first steps of an arduous journey (page 244).

Managing Transitions: Making the Most of Change
by William Bridges (Da Capo Press, 2009)

William Bridges has written our favorite book about change management. It's applicable to all types of change (including culture change), and it is easy to read and understand. Great examples and actionable checklists can be found throughout the book. We appreciate that Bridges keeps the focus on caring about people through the change process.

Before you can begin something new, you have to end what used to be. Before you can learn a new way of doing things, you have to unlearn the old way…. So beginnings depend on endings. The problem is, people don't like endings (page 23).

The Advantage: Why Organizational Health Trumps Everything Else in Business
by Patrick Lencioni (Jossey-Bass, 2012)

This book provides guidance for workplaces that wish to develop their competitive advantage through organizational health. Lencioni provides case studies from organizations he has consulted with, and whose successes and failures illustrate the importance and application of the book's principles. The section on creating organizational values is one of the most clear and helpful guides on the subject we've read.

> *A good way to recognize health is to look for the signs that indicate an organization has it. These include minimal politics and confusion, high degrees of morale and productivity, and very low turnover among good employees.... Whenever I list these qualities for leaders ... often they laugh quietly, in a nervous, almost guilty kind of way* (page 5).

The Best Place to Work: The Art and Science of Creating an Extraordinary Workplace
by Ron Friedman (Penguin, 2015)

Ron Friedman's book reveals why so many employees are dissatisfied with their workplaces and offers suggestions for changing these things. For those who appreciate heavily researched and referenced writing, Friedman draws on numerous sources to explain his conclusions. We especially like the "Action Items for Managers" at the end of each chapter. These points offer a blueprint for how to implement these ideas in your workplace.

> *When we fulfill employees' needs for autonomy, competence, and relatedness, when we allow them to leverage the full breadth of their mental capacity ... we achieve more than an extraordinary workplace. We create an organization that performs at its very best* (page 274).

The Man Who Lied to His Laptop: What Machines Teach Us About Human Relationships
by Clifford Nass with Corina Yen (Penguin, 2010)

This book explores how people interact with their computers to help us understand the nature of human social interactions. It is divided into five easy-to-read chapters: "Praise and Criticism," "Personality," "Teams and Team Building," "Emotion," and "Persuasion." Nass and Yen's writing style is both humorous and research based. We like that the book is full of practical and easy-to-implement ideas that have the potential to positively impact any workplace culture.

> *By bringing together people with very different views and highlighting that you have brought them together specifically to benefit from their diverse knowledge, you combat the idea that being a team means agreeing with each other* (page 109).

The Ordinary Leader: 10 Key Insights for Building and Leading a Thriving Organization
by Randy Grieser (ACHIEVE Publishing, 2017)

We love stories about building something special, and this book is just that. It is our story, the story of how our own company was built. Throughout the book, I, Randy, present my observations about leadership and culture in an accessible way. The chapters on organizational health and employee engagement are particularly helpful in their relation to the importance of workplace culture. The "Questions for Reflection" sections at the end of each chapter make this an ideal book to read in a leadership development book club.

> *Employees want to be part of something bigger than their tasks. Leaders must help employees find a sense of purpose in their work that goes beyond simply completing their everyday responsibilities. Employees will participate and even excel in these less than desirable roles if they believe their work is connected to a greater purpose* (page 25).

Resources

The resources in this section provide more detailed guidance and examples for putting the ideas presented in this book into action. We've mentioned each resource in one of the preceding chapters. At the top of each resource, the chapter and page number(s) are referenced so you can more easily go back and re-read the related sections. Additionally, you can find these resources as downloadable PDFs on our website at www.achievecentre.com.

PURPOSE AND VALUES QUESTIONNAIRE
Referenced in Chapter 2, page 34.

This resource is a guide to help leaders facilitate discussions about purpose and values.

Organizational Purpose Questions
1. How are we making the world a better place?
2. Why do we exist? What would be lost if we didn't exist?
3. What are we trying to achieve in the big picture?

Team Purpose Questions
1. What is the work of our team, and why does it matter?
2. What would be lost if we didn't exist as a team?
3. How are we contributing to the work of other teams and the organization's purpose as a whole?

Organizational Values Questions
1. When our organization is at its best, what behaviors do we see?
2. Which behaviors or ways of acting are so important that we would ask someone to leave if they didn't live them out?
3. Which behaviors are so important that we wouldn't apologize for them, even if a potential client or customer didn't like them?

Consider the Results
After everyone involved has had a chance to contribute to the conversation, work to sharpen the initial ideas. Avoid the temptation to use generic language. Instead, focus on expressing purpose and values in ways that are specific to the culture of your organization. The final statements should resonate with everyone across your organization.

SAMPLE INTERVIEW QUESTIONS

Referenced in Chapter 3, page 40.

Here is a sample of the types of questions we typically ask candidates. We use the first list of questions to help us consider whether a candidate is a good fit for our culture. The second list helps us assess their talent and aptitude. While some of the questions are not explicitly about purpose, values, talents, or aptitude, they are sometimes the most useful questions for helping assess for fit.

Purpose, Values, and Culture Questions

1. Do you have friends at work?
2. When will we hear you laugh?
3. Tell us about a time when someone said something that really bothered you. What was your response?
4. What annoys you at work? What makes you happy at work?
5. Tell us about a time when you received feedback that was difficult to hear.
6. When you read our statement of values, what stands out to you? Why?
7. Please provide examples of how you align with our values.
8. Our organization's purpose is to_____. How does that connect with what you care about?

Talent and Aptitude Questions

1. What kinds of activities or roles come easily for you?
2. What types of things do you learn quickly?
3. What was your favorite course or area of study in school? What did you like least?
4. When you look back at the end of a work day or week, what makes you feel good about what you accomplished?
5. As you think about your last position, what kinds of work tasks or responsibilities did you like the least?
6. What activities or roles bring you a sense of satisfaction?
7. What do your friends or family members appreciate about you?
8. What are your hobbies and interests?

A GUIDE FOR BUILDING CONSENSUS

Referenced in Chapter 6, page 128.

Using consensus to make decisions can be one of the more challenging forms of decision making to do well. Here is a guide for helping you use consensus as a decision making process.

Basic Principles

- Differences of opinion should be encouraged in early stages of discussion.
- The facilitator should assume that silence means disagreement, not agreement.
- Everyone must feel they have been heard.
- The group should make a reasonable effort to address every concern raised about the proposal under consideration.
- As a minimum, each person must be able to "live with" the decision that is made.
- Everyone must agree to support the decision once it is made.

Reaching Consensus

The following are examples of how a formal or informal consensus process might proceed after discussion about issues and proposals:

Informal consensus

- The facilitator asks if anyone has further concerns with the proposal at hand.
- They then look at each person and provide time to respond.
- The facilitator declares that a consensus has been reached if no further concerns are raised.

Formal consensus

- The facilitator asks if anyone has further significant concerns that must be addressed in order for them to support the proposal.
- They then ask each person to verbally respond with one of the following four options:
  1. Yes.
  2. Yes, and … (I wish that, or I'd like to add that…).
  3. Yes, but … (I have significant concerns to be recorded in the minutes. However, I am prepared to support the decision).
  4. No.

If Someone Is Blocking Consensus

- Ensure that their reason for blocking is clearly understood by everyone.
- Ensure that the person blocking has participated fully in the whole session.
- Ask the person blocking to offer an alternative or compromise.
- Break the proposal into sections, and reach consensus on one issue at a time.
- Sleep on it and revisit the issue at a later date.

CONFLICT TRANSFORMATION GUIDE

Referenced in Chapter 7, page 142.

This is a brief summary of the steps required to manage and transform conflict. Both employees and leaders can refer back to this guide when involved in conflict.

Level 1: Engage in Direct Discussion

Focus: using conflict resolution skills.

Action: talk directly with the other person.

Level 2: Recognize Thinking Errors

Focus: extending grace to yourself *and* the other person.

Action: talk with the other person about the issues, not their character.

Level 3: Provide Conflict Resolution Coaching

Focus: improving your approach through coaching.

Action: talk with the other person again using an improved approach.

Level 4: Use a Conflict Resolution Specialist

Focus: finding mutual support for conflict resolution.

Action: talk with the other person using a specialist's assistance.

Level 5: Change Relationships

Focus: finding ways to change or end relationships and build new relational structures.

Action: talk as needed without enmity.

CONFLICT MANAGEMENT & RESPECTFUL WORKPLACE GUIDELINES

Referenced in Chapter 7, page 144.

ACHIEVE uses this resource internally as a guide for resolving conflict and maintaining a respectful workplace. We encourage you to consider elements of these guidelines as you review or create your own.

Conflict Resolution

We believe that conflict is unavoidable. It is inherent within all organizations and groups. How we handle conflict determines whether it is destructive or constructive. Conflict is not the same as disrespect, although people may behave disrespectfully while in conflict. There are many sources of conflict, including disagreements, personality clashes, and differences of opinion. Constructive conflict resolution becomes easier when we share a high level of trust, believe the best about each other, and commit to listening to each other. We work to resolve our conflicts constructively because that creates a relational environment in which we can reach our goals as an organization.

Respectful Workplace

We believe that disrespect is any type of behavior that causes offense to someone else. This includes behavior like putting others down, verbal abuse, avoiding, ignoring, excluding, or bullying others, and using negative body language. Respect, on the other hand, is when people treat each other with consideration and empathy. Respect encompasses more than just showing restraint and putting up with certain people or behaviors. When people respect each other, they safeguard the dignity of their coworkers. Respect also entails welcoming differences and recognizing that they contribute to a vibrant workplace.

Focus on Impact

When it comes to issues of respect and conflict, it is the impact of our actions that matter, not our intentions. An individual may have no intent to be disrespectful, but if he or she is perceived as disrespectful, then the behavior is disrespectful. If our intent was not malicious but the effect was negative, we must acknowledge, apologize for, and change our behavior, even when we meant no harm.

Approaching Disrespect and Conflict

When tensions around disrespect or conflict arise in the workplace, let the following principles guide you.

Before doing anything, remember:

1. Most people do not act with poor intentions, so when you are feeling badly about something someone has done or said, assume that they probably did not mean to hurt you.
2. Most people want to be approached directly when someone else has a concern about something they have done or said.
3. Email and social media are very poor ways to address disrespect and conflict. They typically only escalate the situation. Address issues in person, or if that is not possible, over the phone.

Starting a conversation:

1. Most people prefer to be asked about their actions first rather than being told that their actions did not work. So start with a question about what was behind a certain action. For example, say, "I'm curious about what you meant when you said…"
2. Listen – try to understand.
3. If necessary, share how a person's actions affected you, as well as what you would prefer that person to have said or done.

Always remember:

1. Ask if there would be a better time to talk.
2. Suggest bringing in another person to help the conversation (a peer or manager).
3. Approach your team leader for confidential coaching on how to handle the situation. Note that a manager will not generally convey a message on your behalf. Instead, they will help you figure out what to say or do, or they will hold a joint meeting to help everyone talk.

CULTURAL HEALTH ASSESSMENT

Referenced in Chapter 8, page 164.

This abbreviated Cultural Health Assessment tool assists leaders in evaluating and understanding organizational culture. It is useful for generating engaging and proactive discussions within groups. A complete assessment tool package, including a facilitator's guide and 25 copies of the full questionnaire, is available on our website at www.achievecentre.com.

Instructions

Review the statements below and rate each statement on a scale of 1 to 5. A 5 indicates you strongly agree with the statement; a 1 indicates you strongly disagree with the statement.

___1. Leaders in my organization clearly communicate its purpose.

___2. I have the freedom to choose how best to accomplish my work.

___3. My manager asks for my opinions on work-related decisions.

___4. My colleagues care about my well-being.

___5. Information is shared openly and effectively across departments.

___6. I am treated with respect.

___7. People understand what behaviors are acceptable in the workplace.

___8. Most of the work I do is interesting and challenging to me.

___9. I have a good relationship with my direct supervisor.

___10. I like the people I work with.

___11. Teamwork is encouraged and valued.

___12. Conflict is minimal and, if it arises, is managed quickly and effectively.

Considering the Results

Statements that are rated 1 or 2 should be viewed with concern, particularly when that result is seen in more than one survey. Organizational leaders should focus their attention on resolving these issues quickly. Ratings of 3 may indicate an area that should be watched or given secondary attention. Ratings of 4 or 5 should be celebrated.

CULTURE CHANGE GUIDE

Referenced in Chapter 8, page 162.

This resource is a guide for helping organizations work through culture change.

Phase 1: Assess Your Current Culture

- Observe social interactions. How do people interact with each other?
- Observe emotions. Do you notice tension, discomfort, laughter, etc.?
- Assess the physical environment. Is the workspace welcoming and inviting for everyone?
- Talk to people. Ask questions like these:
  - "How would you respond if a friend asked you, 'What's it like to work in your organization?'"
  - "What are the best things about the way we do our work?"
  - "How would you describe the relational atmosphere of our organization?"
  - "What is the main thing you'd like to see changed in our organization?"

Phase 2: Envision a Desired Culture

- Interview people from other organizations you respect.
- Meet again with the people you talked to in Phase 1. Ask them for suggestions.
- Convene joint meetings between your culture change team and senior leaders. Together, consider which of the six main elements of healthy workplace culture need attention:
  - Communicating your purpose and values
  - Providing meaningful work
  - Focusing your leadership team on people
  - Building meaningful relationships
  - Creating peak performing teams
  - Practicing constructive conflict management

- Taking each of these areas into account, draft a concise and readable document that describes a concrete vision for your organization's culture. Include clear goals, expected milestones, and a schedule for evaluation.

Phase 3: Share and Teach the Culture
- Set up departmental meetings to present your culture change document and discuss the following:
  - Why changes are being made.
  - How changes are being made.
  - When changes are happening.
  - Who is responsible for making the changes.
  - How you will know when you have successfully changed.
- Offer training for identified problem areas.

Phase 4: Monitor and Provide Accountability
- Periodically check in and assess how things are going. Use the same strategies from Phase 1.

Key Points to Remember
- Make small, easy, and simple changes *now*.
- Risk *over*-communicating rather than *under*-communicating.

References

Introduction

1. "The Culture Question Survey," ACHIEVE Centre for Leadership & Workplace Performance, 2018, www.achieve-publishing.com/wp-content/uploads/2018/09/Culture-Question-Survey-Analysis.pdf.

CHAPTER 1   The Case for Caring About Culture

1. Boris Groysberg, Jeremiah Lee, Jesse Price, and J. Yo-Jud Cheng, "The Leader's Guide to Corporate Culture," *Harvard Business Review*, January 2018, www.hbr.org/2018/01/the-culture-factor.
2. "How Corporate Culture Affects the Bottom Line," Fuqua School of Business, November 12, 2015, www.fuqua.duke.edu/news_events/news-releases/corporate-culture/.

CHAPTER 2   Communicate Your Purpose & Values

1. Simon Sinek, "How Great Leaders Inspire Action," filmed September 2009 in Puget Sound, WA, TEDx video, 17:58, www.ted.com/talks/simon_sinek_how_great_leaders_inspire_action.
2. Tony Hsieh, *Delivering Happiness: A Path to Profits, Passion, and Purpose* (New York: Business Plus, 2010), 107.
3. Nick Craig and Scott A. Snook, "From Purpose to Impact," *Harvard Business Review*, May 2014, www.hbr.org/2014/05/from-purpose-to-impact.
4. Patrick Lencioni, *The Advantage: Why Organizational Health Trumps Everything Else in Business* (San Francisco: Jossey-Bass, 2012), 91–104.

CHAPTER 3   Provide Meaningful Work

1. "ACHIEVE Personality Dimensions Assessment," ACHIEVE Centre for Leadership & Workplace Performance, 2018.

2. Frederick Herzberg, "One More Time: How Do You Motivate Employees?," *Harvard Business Review*, January 1968. Republished January 2003, www.hbr.org/2003/01/one-more-time-how-do-you-motivate-employees.

3. Daniel H. Pink, *Drive: The Surprising Truth About What Motivates Us* (New York: Riverhead Books, 2009), 11.

4. Ron Friedman, *The Best Place to Work: The Art and Science of Creating an Extraordinary Workplace* (New York: Penguin, 2015), 142–3.

5. *I Love Lucy*, "Job Switching," Season 2, Episode 1, Directed by William Asher. Written by Bob Carroll Jr., Jess Oppenheimer, and Madelyn Davis. CBS, September 15, 1952.

6. Mihaly Csikszentmihalyi, *Flow: The Psychology of Optimal Experience* (New York: Harper & Row, 1990), 154.

CHAPTER 4   Focus Your Leadership Team on People

1. Sigal G. Barsade and Olivia A. O'Neill, "What's Love Got to Do with It? A Longitudinal Study of the Culture of Companionate Love and Employee and Client Outcomes in a Long-term Care Setting," *Administrative Science Quarterly* 54, no. 4 (May 2014): 551–98.

2. Natalia M. Lorinkova, Matthew J. Pearsall, and Henry P. Sims, "Examining the Differential Longitudinal Performance of Directive versus Empowering Leadership in Teams," *Academy of Management Journal* 56, no. 2 (May 2012): 573.

3. Ibid.

4. Jack Zenger and Joseph Folkman, "The Ideal Praise-to-Criticism Ratio," *Harvard Business Review*, March 15, 2013, www.hbr.org/2013/03/the-ideal-praise-to-criticism.

5. Clifford Nass with Corina Yen, *The Man Who Lied to His Laptop: What Machines Teach Us About Human Relationships* (New York: Penguin Group, 2010), 38.

6. Ted Wachtel, "Defining Restorative," International Institute for Restorative Practices, 2016, www.iirp.edu/images/pdf/Defining-Restorative_Nov-2016.pdf.

7. Daniel H. Pink, *Drive: The Surprising Truth About What Motivates Us* (New York: Riverhead Books, 2009), 71.

CHAPTER 5 Build Meaningful Relationships

1. Scott Berinato, "What Do We Know About Loneliness and Work?" *Harvard Business Review*, September 28, 2017, www.hbr.org/2017/09/what-do-we-know-about-loneliness-and-work.

2. Richard Sheridan, *Joy, Inc.: How We Built a Workplace People Love* (New York: Penguin, 2015), 22.

3. Priyanka B. Carr and Gregory M. Walton, "Cues of Working Together Fuel Intrinsic Motivation," *Journal of Experimental Social Psychology*, no. 53 (July 2014): 169–84.

4. Scott Berinato, "What Do We Know About Loneliness and Work?" *Harvard Business Review*, September 28, 2017, www.hbr.org/2017/09/what-do-we-know-about-loneliness-and-work.

5. Jessica R. Methot, Jeffery A. Lepine, Nathan P. Podsakoff, and Jessica Siegel Christian, "Are Workplace Friendships a Mixed Blessing? Exploring Tradeoffs of Multiplex Relationships and Their Associations with Job Performance," *Personnel Psychology* 69, no. 2 (2015): 1–45.

6. Irving L. Janis, "Groupthink." *Psychology Today* 5, no. 6 (November 1971): 84–90.

7. Peggy Drexler, "The Truth About Office Romance," *Forbes*, April 7, 2014, www.forbes.com/sites/peggydrexler/2014/04/07/the-truth-about-office-romance/#599e1e416673.

CHAPTER 6 Create Peak Performing Teams

1. Francis Galton, "Vox Populi," *Nature* 75, no. 1949 (1907): 450–51, www.galton.org/essays/1900-1911/galton-1907-vox-populi.pdf?page=7.

2. Diane Coutu, "Why Teams Don't Work," *Harvard Business Review*, May 2009, www.hbr.org/2009/05/why-teams-dont-work.

3. Noah J. Goldstein, Robert B. Cialdini, and Vladas Griskevicius, "A Room with a Viewpoint: Using Social Norms to Motivate Environmental Conservation in Hotels," *Journal of Consumer Research* 35, no. 3 (October 2008): 472–482.

4. Morten T. Hansen, *Great at Work: How Top Performers Do Less, Work Better, and Achieve More* (New York: Simon & Schuster, 2018), 138.

5. James K. Esser and Joanne S. Lindoerfer, "Groupthink and the Space Shuttle Challenger Accident: Toward a Quantitative Case Analysis," *Journal of Behavioral Decision Making* 2, no. 3, (July 1989): 167–77.

CHAPTER 7 Practice Constructive Conflict Management

1. "Warring Egos, Toxic Individuals, Feeble Leadership: A Study of Conflict in the Canadian Workplace," Psychometrics Canada Ltd, 2009, www.psychometrics.com/wp-content/uploads/2015/04/conflictstudy_09.pdf.

2. "Workplace Conflict and How Businesses Can Harness It to Thrive," CPP, Inc., 2008, https://img.en25.com/Web/CPP/Conflict_report.pdf.

3. John Paul Lederach, *The Little Book of Conflict Transformation: Clear Articulation of the Guiding Principles by a Pioneer in the Field* (Intercourse, PA: Good Books. 2003).

4. *The Anatomy of Peace: Resolving the Heart of Conflict*, The Arbinger Institute (Oakland: Berrett-Koehler Publishers, Inc., 2015), 58.

5. "ACHIEVE Personality Dimensions Assessment," ACHIEVE Centre for Leadership & Workplace Performance, 2018.

6. Stephen B. Karpman, "Fairy Tales and Script Drama Analysis," *Transactional Analysis Bulletin* 7, no. 26 (1968): 39–43.

CHAPTER 8 How to Change Culture

1. "Global Human Capital Trends 2016: The New Organization: Different by Design," Deloitte University Press, 2016, www2.deloitte.com/content/dam/Deloitte/global/Documents/HumanCapital/gx-dup-global-human-capital-trends-2016.pdf.

2. S. Chris Edmonds, *The Culture Engine: A Framework for Driving Results, Inspiring Your Employees, and Transforming Your Workplace* (Hoboken: John Wiley & Sons, Inc., 2014), 12.

3. John P. Kotter, "Leading Change: Why Transformation Efforts Fail," *Harvard Business Review*, January 2007, www.hbr.org/2007/01/leading-change-why-transformation-efforts-fail.

4. William Bridges, *Managing Transitions: Making the Most of Change* (Philadelphia: Da Capo Press, 2009).

5. Roger Connors and Tom Smith, *Change the Culture, Change the Game: The Breakthrough Strategy for Energizing Your Organization and Creating Accountability for Results* (New York: Penguin, 2011), 113.

Acknowledgments

We are thankful for the many people who have assisted in bringing this book to completion. This project has been the work of many hands.

In particular, we want to thank Tyler Voth, ACHIEVE's internal editor, who read and provided feedback on the manuscript at every step along the way. In addition, we want to acknowledge the role of Micah Zerbe, who analyzed our survey responses and wrote the first draft of the book's Survey Analysis section.

Thank you to Marion Brown, Heidi Grieser, Ana Speranza, and John VanWalleghem, who read and provided feedback on the manuscript. We are grateful for the skill and watchful eye of our editor Tim Runtz, and for our proofreaders Jessica Antony and Ardell Stauffer. A big thank you to Lisa Friesen. Her creativity resulted in a fabulous book cover and interior design.

We want to express our appreciation to the 2,401 people who participated in our survey. Your responses provided rich material for our book. We thank you for sharing your insights and opinions.

Finally, we are eternally grateful to our families who supported us in many different ways as we wrote this book. Thank you for your thoughtfulness and patience. We love you.

Speaking and Training

For your next conference, convention, or leadership retreat, consider having Randy, Eric, Wendy, or Michael as your speaker. Each of them provides engaging, inspirational, and humorous keynotes as well as workshops and retreats.

ACHIEVE Centre for Leadership & Workplace Performance provides workshops on over 40 topics in the areas of leadership development and workplace performance. The Crisis & Trauma Resource Institute offers more than 50 workshop topics in the areas of counseling, mental health, and violence prevention. Options for accessing training include:

Public Workshops

Open enrollment workshops are offered throughout the year in many locations. Visit our website to find out which workshops are being offered near you.

On-site Training

Training is offered on location – right where you work. If you have a group of people to train, on-site training is often the most cost-effective and convenient way to obtain training.

Webinars and Live Streaming

No matter where you live, you can easily access one-hour webinars and full-day live streaming workshops right from your desk.

For more information:

www.achievecentre.com
info@achievecentre.com
877-270-9776

www.ctrinstitute.com
info@ctrinstitute.com
877-353-3205